JUMBO
BIBLE
CHRISTMAS
Activity & Trivia Fun

SHILOH ♪ kidz

An Imprint of Barbour Publishing, Inc.

ISBN 978-1-64352-104-6

Published by Shiloh Kidz, an imprint of Barbour Publishing, Inc., 1810 Barbour Drive, Uhrichsville, Ohio 44683, www.shilohkidz.com

Our mission is to inspire the world with the life-changing message of the Bible.

Member of the
Evangelical Christian
Publishers Association

Printed in the United States of America.
06668 0819 BP

WISE MEN TRIVIA

INTRODUCTION

Welcome to this one-of-a-kind book about the Wise Men of the Bible. This section contains 30 quizzes with 12 questions in each one. If you answer 9 to 12 questions in a quiz correctly, you're definitely a Wise Man (or a Wise Woman)! If you answer 5 to 8 questions correctly, you're a Wise Guy. . .keep working at it. If you answer 0 to 4 questions correctly, well, it's time to get back to the books—specifically, *the* Book, the Bible.

God's Word is the source of the greatest knowledge and wisdom in the world—so don't miss out. His truths "are not just idle words for you—they are your life" (Deuteronomy 32:47 NIV). They are not only vitally important for your spiritual life, but they're also very interesting. And as you are about to see, learning about them can be a great deal of fun.

1

THE WISE MEN

In the Nativity story, Matthew tells us about the arrival of mysterious visitors from somewhere in the East. Some legends say their names were Melchior, Caspar, and Balthazar, and that they were three kings of distant lands. In the original Greek, Matthew calls them "magi," which means they were part of a special group of wise men and priests. Some Bible translations simply call them the Wise Men, and perhaps that's the best title of all.

In ancient days, people went to wise men and women for advice when they had difficult choices to make. Ancient kings *often* faced difficult decisions—sometimes every day!—so they kept a group of wise men with them full-time. Kings in the Bible did this as well. There were many wise men and women in the Bible, whether they lived in the royal court or in their own villages where ordinary people could seek their advice.

1. What wise man did Pharaoh put in charge of all the land of Egypt?
   a) Potiphar
   b) Moses
   c) Joseph
   d) Einstein

2. When he was young, Moses studied all the wisdom of _____.
   a) the Israelites
   b) the Babylonians
   c) the Hebrews
   d) the Egyptians

3. Moses' father-in-law gave Moses very wise advice. What was his name?
   a) Jethro
   b) Adam
   c) Caiaphas
   d) Solomon

4. What was the name of the wise woman who stopped David from taking revenge?
   a) Hannah
   b) Bathsheba
   c) Abigail
   d) Michelle

5. Which ancient Israelite king was famous for his great wisdom?
   a) Solomon
   b) Methuselah
   c) Aaron
   d) Saul

6. Which superrich Israelite king was wiser than Ethan, Heman, Chalcol, and Darda?
   a) Hezekiah
   b) Josiah
   c) Zedekiah
   d) Solomon

7. God gave Daniel and his friends knowledge and skill in _____.
   a) video games
   b) all literature and wisdom
   c) Israelite history
   d) ducks and geese

8. Job's wise friends gave him lots of not-so-wise advice. Where did Job live?
   a) Oz
   b) Uz
   c) Az
   d) Iz

9. The book of Proverbs says that Wisdom was with God in the
_____.
 a) treasures of snow
 b) midst of the desert
 c) depth of the seas
 d) beginning

10. A wise woman was married to a man named Nabal. What kind of
man was Nabal?
 a) foolish
 b) wise
 c) neighborly
 d) generous

11. Jesus said that a foolish man builds his house upon the sand, but
that a wise man builds his house upon the _____.
 a) sand
 b) cement foundation
 c) wooden posts
 d) rock

12. The Bible says, "If any of you lacks _____, let him ask of God. . .
and it will be given to him."
 a) money
 b) wisdom
 c) hugs
 d) candy bars

ANSWERS

1. c) Joseph (Genesis 41:39–41)
2. d) the Egyptians (Acts 7:22)
3. a) Jethro (Exodus 18:5, 13–24)
4. c) Abigail (1 Samuel 25:32–33)
5. a) Solomon (1 Kings 10:23)
6. d) Solomon (1 Kings 4:29–31)
7. b) all literature and wisdom (Daniel 1:6, 17 NKJV)
8. b) Uz (Job 1:1)
9. d) beginning (Proverbs 8:12, 22–24)
10. a) foolish (1 Samuel 25:25)
11. d) rock (Matthew 7:24–25)
12. b) wisdom (James 1:5 NKJV)

How well did you do on these questions about the wise (and not-so-wise) people of the Bible? If you got most of the answers right, congratulations! You were obviously paying attention in church and Sunday school—and that's a wise thing to do.

If you got some of the answers wrong, don't worry. Wise men and women learn from their mistakes, and become even smarter. As King Solomon said, "A wise man will hear and increase learning" (Proverbs 1:5 NKJV). Solomon also said, "Give instruction to a wise man, and he will be still wiser. . .and he will increase in learning" (Proverbs 9:9 NKJV). So tune in to learning—at home, in school, and in church—and you'll end up wiser than you already are!

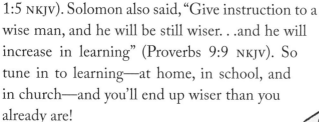

2

PEOPLE OF PERSIA

Matthew 2:1 tells us that the Wise Men came from the East. According to Christian tradition, they were from Persia, Arabia, and India. Modern Christmas plays often show characters from Europe, Arabia, and Africa. Actually, the Wise Men most likely all came from one country (see Matthew 2:12). Which country? Probably Persia. Wise men called "magi" were from there.

In Jesus' day Persia was the heart of the Parthian Empire, to the east of Israel. At one point, almost all Jews lived there. At the time of the first Christmas, hundreds of thousands of Jews still called Parthia home. In the book of Acts, Luke listed many faraway places Jews had come from to attend the feast of Pentecost, and the first was Parthia (Acts 2:8–9). The Persians and Parthians played a big role in the Bible.

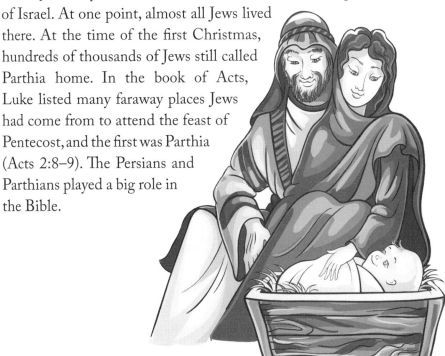

1. Cyrus, king of Persia, freed the Jews and told them to go to Jerusalem to build a _____.
   a) train station
   b) house (temple) for God
   c) palace for the high priest
   d) tree house

2. What did the jealous Persian governors trick King Darius into doing?
   a) chopping down the Royal Forest
   b) throwing Jonah into the sea
   c) throwing Daniel into the lions' den
   d) throwing Jeremiah into a muddy pit

3. God showed Daniel that the kings of Media and Persia were like a _____.
   a) two-horned ram
   b) winged lion
   c) triceratops
   d) bulldog

4. The evening that Darius conquered Babylon, what was the king of Babylon doing?
   a) sleeping in his bed
   b) enjoying a great feast
   c) combing his royal horses
   d) leading his army in battle

5. This man led the first group of Jews back from Persia to Jerusalem.
   a) Zadok
   b) Zerubbabel
   c) Zechariah
   d) Zebedee

6. King Artaxerxes told his officials to give Ezra all he could possibly use of _____.
   a) gold
   b) sugar
   c) salt
   d) paper

7. This brave cupbearer led the Jews to rebuild the broken walls of Jerusalem.
   a) Nehemiah
   b) Nahum
   c) St. Francis
   d) Bob the Builder

8. Ezra read the Book of the Law while standing on top of _____.
   a) an elephant
   b) the temple steps
   c) a wooden platform
   d) a moving oxcart

9. Which beautiful Jewish woman was chosen to marry the king of Persia?

    a) Judith
    b) Bathsheba
    c) the queen of Sheba
    d) Esther

10. A Jew named Mordecai overheard two men plotting. What were they plotting?

    a) to steal an iPod
    b) to kill all the Jews
    c) to kill the king
    d) to rob the bank

11. This powerful man in the Persian capital was an enemy of the Jews. Who was he?

    a) Haman the Agagite
    b) Doeg the Edomite
    c) Uriah the Hittite
    d) Ittai the Gittite

12. This prophet wrote the last book in the Old Testament after the Jews left the Persian Empire.

    a) Jonah
    b) Isaiah
    c) Ezekiel
    d) Malachi

ANSWERS

1. b) house (temple) for God (Ezra 1:1–3)
2. c) throwing Daniel into the lions' den (Daniel 6:1–23)
3. a) two-horned ram (Daniel 8:20)
4. b) enjoying a great feast (Daniel 5:1, 30–31)
5. b) Zerubbabel (Ezra 2:1–2)
6. c) salt (Ezra 7:21–22)
7. a) Nehemiah (Nehemiah 1:1, 11; 2:17–18)
8. c) a wooden platform (Nehemiah 8:3–4 NKJV)
9. d) Esther (Esther 2:17)
10. c) to kill the king (Esther 2:21–23)
11. a) Haman the Agagite
    (Esther 3:1, 10)
12. d) Malachi (Malachi 1:1)

How did you do on these questions about famous men and women of the Persian Empire? Did you have any idea that the Persians played such an important role in the Bible? If your Bible has maps in the back, why not flip through those pages and see if you can find Persia or Parthia?

God had a special relationship with His chosen people, the Jews, and He inspired several of the wise kings of Persia to help them in great ways. The most famous example was King Cyrus. God named Cyrus before he was even born and said that Cyrus would set His people free and allow them to rebuild Jerusalem and the temple (see Isaiah 44:24–28; 45:1–4, 13).

The Persians had a long history of blessing God's people. It was truly fitting that the Wise Men probably came from that land.

3

THE STAR OF BETHLEHEM

So the Wise Men were probably somewhere in the Parthian Empire, giving out wise advice and studying to be even wiser, when one night they looked up and saw a bright star in the western sky, in the direction of Israel. They'd never seen it before, and it was so outstanding that they knew something very important had just happened in Israel.

Ever since then, people have tried to figure out what the Star of Bethlehem was. Some guess that it was a comet. Others speculate that a supernova (a bright, exploding star) suddenly appeared. Others think that a "star" was created when two planets, Jupiter and Saturn, passed close to each other. Many Christians believe that the Christmas Star was a special miracle.

But this amazing star isn't the only one the Bible mentions. See how much you know about some heavenly bodies that are mentioned in scripture.

1. Which Bible book describes God creating the stars, the sun, and the moon?
   a) Matthew
   b) Ruth
   c) Genesis
   d) Revelation

2. God told Abraham to look up at the stars and try to do an impossible thing. It was to _____.
   a) blow out all their lights
   b) count them all
   c) name them all
   d) make his cow jump over the moon

3. In teen Joseph's dream, what did the sun, the moon, and eleven stars do?
   a) suddenly stopped shining
   b) began to dance
   c) began to sing
   d) bowed down to him

4. While living forty years in the desert, the _____ worshiped the star of a false god.
   a) Israelites
   b) Canaanites
   c) Amalekites
   d) Jebusites

5. During a famous battle, Joshua commanded _____ to stand still.
   a) the sun and the stars
   b) the sun and the moon
   c) the moon and the stars
   d) the sun, the moon, and the stars

6. The book of Judges says that the stars fought against _____ and his armies.
   a) Caesar Augustus
   b) Barak
   c) the Dragon
   d) Sisera

7. Instead of eating with King Saul on the New Moon feast, what did David do?
   a) hid in the field
   b) fasted
   c) sat at the table and stared
   d) ate at McDonald's

8. When you look up and see the sun, the moon, and the stars, what are you not to do?
   a) admire their beauty
   b) look at them with telescopes
   c) worship them
   d) stare till they blind you

9. The foolish kings of Judah worshiped the sun and built _____ for it.
   a) houses
   b) swimming pools
   c) landing pads
   d) chariots

10. Daniel wrote that people who _____ will shine like the stars forever.
   a) lead many to righteousness
   b) get all A's in school
   c) never sin
   d) fast and pray

11. Jesus told John that the seven stars in His right hand symbolized _____.
   a) seven churches
   b) seven world empires
   c) seven angels
   d) seven movie stars

12. Isaiah prophesied that in the end times the stars will fall from the sky like _____.
   a) thousand-pound hailstones
   b) figs from a fig tree
   c) cats and dogs
   d) a swarm of locusts

ANSWERS

1. c) Genesis (Genesis 1:14–19)
2. b) count them all (Genesis 15:5)
3. d) bowed down to him (Genesis 37:9 NKJV)
4. a) Israelites (Amos 5:25–26)
5. b) the sun and the moon (Joshua 10:12)
6. d) Sisera (Judges 5:19–20)
7. a) hid in the field (1 Samuel 20:5, 24–25)
8. c) worship them (Deuteronomy 4:19; 17:2–5)
9. d) chariots (2 Kings 23:11)
10. a) lead many to righteousness (Daniel 12:3 NLT)
11. c) seven angels (Revelation 1:20)
12. b) figs from a fig tree (Isaiah 34:4 NIV)

Now, what do you think the Christmas Star was? (a) a comet, (b) a supernova, (c) two very close planets, or (d) a special miracle? Well, God *could* have used one of the first three choices, except for the unusual things the star did. When the Wise Men left Jerusalem "the star which they had seen in the East went before them, till it came and stood over where the young Child was" (Matthew 2:9 NKJV).

The star "went before them" as they rode five miles to Bethlehem then stopped *over* the very house where Jesus was. It couldn't have been millions of miles away in space or it would've appeared "over" Jerusalem as much as Bethlehem. That would've been no help. Whatever the star was, God miraculously designed it to lead the Magi.

4

THE WISE MEN AND ASTROLOGY

Many people believe that the Wise Men were astrologers and that they interpreted astrological signs—a new star at a certain place in the zodiac—to figure out that a great king had been born in Israel. They think that astrology is true and that God used it. However, it's important to remember that in the centuries before this, God condemned astrology and warned people to pay no attention to it at all.

Remember also that there were many Jews living in Persia then, and Jewish scribes knew this prophecy: "A star will come out of Jacob; a [king's] scepter will rise out of Israel" (Numbers 24:17 NIV). After they saw the star in the west over Israel, it would've been a simple thing for the *Persian* wise men to learn from the *Jewish* wise men that a star signaled the birth of the long-awaited King of the Jews.

1. Jeremiah warned, "Do not act like the other nations, who try to read their future in _____."
   a) tea leaves
   b) a crystal ball
   c) the stars
   d) palm reading

2. Isaiah said that the counsel people received from astrologers had _____.
   a) only worn them out
   b) made them very wise
   c) helped them make decisions
   d) been lots of fun

3. The magicians, enchanters, and astrologers couldn't interpret Nebuchadnezzar's _____.
   a) handwriting
   b) riddle
   c) foreign language
   d) dream

4. What other useless things did foolish people in Bible times believe in?
   a) the Great Pumpkin
   b) lottery tickets
   c) worshiping idols
   d) lucky rabbit's feet

5. Jesus said that pagans thought their prayers would be answered because they _____.
   a) washed their faces twice a day
   b) repeated their words many times
   c) walked on hot coals
   d) had tattoos all over their bodies

6. God warned that He'd be *against* anyone who turned to _____ for advice.
   a) politicians
   b) lawyers
   c) cousins
   d) mediums

7. King Manasseh practiced _____, and the Lord said that was evil.
   a) the accordion and drums
   b) sorcery and witchcraft
   c) rolling dice
   d) square dancing

8. Many people consider _____ harmless fun, but God has specifically forbidden it.
   a) fortune-telling
   b) watching television
   c) playing baseball
   d) eating ice cream

9. Why did one young woman lose her power to tell people's fortunes?
   a) They didn't pay her first.
   b) She didn't buy a psychic's license.
   c) Paul cast the evil spirit out of her.
   d) She wasn't thankful for her "gift."

10. This disgusting practice was sometimes used to make important decisions.
   a) flipping a coin
   b) examining animals' livers
   c) spinning the wheel of fortune
   d) wishing on a falling star

11. What did some women in Judah tie on people's wrists to supposedly help them?
   a) fake wristwatches
   b) chains
   c) wrist guards
   d) magic charms

12. Omens were "signs from the gods." Whom did the king of Babylon get to look for omens?
   a) his army captains
   b) his magicians
   c) his pet baboon
   d) his wife

ANSWERS

1. c) the stars (Jeremiah 10:2 NLT)
2. a) only worn them out (Isaiah 47:13 NIV)
3. d) dream (Daniel 4:4–7)
4. c) worshiping idols (Isaiah 44:9–20)
5. b) repeated their words many times (Matthew 6:7 NLT)
6. d) mediums (Leviticus 20:6)
7. b) sorcery and witchcraft (2 Chronicles 33:6)
8. a) fortune-telling (Leviticus 19:26 NLT)
9. c) Paul cast the evil spirit out of her. (Acts 16:16–18)
10. b) examining animals' livers (Ezekiel 21:21)
11. d) magic charms (Ezekiel 13:18 NKJV)
12. b) his magicians (Ezekiel 21:21 NLT)

Foolish pagans had many strange ways to help them decide what to do or where to go. Often God's people copied these superstitious practices instead of praying for God to guide them. Or if God took awhile to answer, people ran to an astrologer or medium to get some quick advice. King Saul did that once when God wasn't answering him—and it ended in disaster (1 Samuel 28:6–7; 1 Chronicles 10:13).

The Magi may or may not have believed in astrology. We can't say whether they knew any better or not. But God *didn't use* astrology to tell them that the King of the Jews had been born. God simply put on a miraculous light show to get their attention. And God didn't use astrology to show the Wise Men where Jesus was. He brought a "star" down, nice and low, to show them exactly where to go.

5

WE THREE KINGS

In one Christmas carol the Wise Men say, "We three Kings of Orient are." *Orient* means "East," but why *three* kings? Well, Matthew tells us that when they saw Jesus they worshiped Him and "presented gifts to Him: gold, frankincense, and myrrh" (Matthew 2:11 NKJV). The idea that there were *three* Wise Men comes from the three gifts.

But were they kings? Possibly. Centuries earlier, God prophesied: "The Gentiles [nations] shall come to your light, and kings to the brightness of your rising," and, "They shall bring gold and incense, and they shall proclaim the praises of the LORD" (Isaiah 60:3, 6 NKJV). Frankincense is incense, and many Christians believe that, together with the gold they gave, the Magi fulfilled these prophecies.

So, yes, there could have been *three* Wise Men, and yes, they could have been *kings*. The pages of the Bible are, in fact, filled with ancient kings. How much do you know about these rulers?

1. What was Melchizedek, king of Salem, most famous for?
    a) ruling justly and wisely
    b) defeating the Assyrians
    c) blessing Abraham
    d) his long white beard

2. King Ahimelech ruled over only a tiny city in Israel. What city was that?
    a) Shechem
    b) Nineveh
    c) Rome
    d) Disneyland

3. Who was the very first king over all Israel?
    a) David
    b) Saul
    c) Samuel
    d) LeBron James

4. What did Samuel do to show that David was God's choice for king?
    a) shouted it from his rooftop
    b) washed his feet
    c) placed a crown on his head
    d) poured oil on his head

5. In what ways was King Solomon greater than all other kings on the earth?

   a) in the size of his kingdom

   b) in horses and chariots

   c) in riches and wisdom

   d) in Proverbs and Ecclesiastes

6. Zimri was a bad, selfish king. Fortunately, he only ruled Israel for

_____.

   a) seven days

   b) eight weeks

   c) nine months

   d) one year

7. Many kings ruled Judah, but only one queen ruled Judah. What was her name?

   a) Esther

   b) Jezebel

   c) Elizabeth

   d) Athaliah

8. Which king had his men make copies of the proverbs of Solomon?

   a) David

   b) Nebuchadnezzar

   c) Hezekiah

   d) Ivan the Terrible

9. What did King Jehoshaphat send ahead of his army as they marched to battle?
   a) his best archers
   b) singers
   c) a dozen lions
   d) his war chariots

10. Most kings of Judah were buried in the royal tombs. Where was King Manasseh buried?
   a) in a royal tomb
   b) in the cave of Mamre
   c) in the garden of Uzza
   d) in the tomb of Gimli

11. Which king heard the apostle Paul preach the Gospel?
   a) Agrippa
   b) Old King Cole
   c) Solomon
   d) Lawrence of Arabia

12. In the book of Revelation, Jesus is called the King of _____.
   a) Jerusalem
   b) Zion
   c) Peace
   d) Kings

ANSWERS

1. c) blessing Abraham (Genesis 14:18–20)
2. a) Shechem (Judges 9:1–2, 6)
3. b) Saul (1 Samuel 10:17–24)
4. d) poured oil on his head (1 Samuel 16:1, 13)
5. c) in riches and wisdom (2 Chronicles 9:22)
6. a) seven days (1 Kings 16:15)
7. d) Athaliah (2 Kings 11:1–3)
8. c) Hezekiah (Proverbs 25:1)
9. b) singers (2 Chronicles 20:20–24)
10. c) in the garden of Uzza (2 Kings 21:18)
11. a) Agrippa (Acts 26:1–3)
12. d) Kings (Revelation 19:16)

Are you enjoying the questions and answers so far? Are you learning anything new that you didn't already know? In fact, is so much of this information new that you're practically guessing *all* the answers? Guessing or not, how did you score in this last quiz?

A final note about the Three Kings: As you've learned from these questions, some kings in Bible times had very *small* kingdoms. Melchizedek was a super-important, totally unique Bible figure, yet he only ruled over one little hilltop city—Salem. And Ahimelech ruled the tiny town of Shechem. So the Wise Men could have been kings over small cities *within* the Parthian Empire. They didn't have to be rulers over entire countries to be kings.

6

CAMELS AND CARAVANS

Israel was many hundreds of miles from Parthia, and in those days—traveling on plodding camels—such a journey took a couple of months. Did they really need to see Him *personally*? Yes. This newborn child was not only the King of the Jews, but the ancient prophecies said that He would rule over all nations. So the Wise Men set out on a long journey to find and to worship Him.

Since they *were* Wise Men, they knew that it wasn't wise to travel such long distances alone. For safety, merchants and travelers banded together in large, well-organized caravans. So the Magi put together their own caravan or (more likely) joined a large caravan that was already headed that direction.

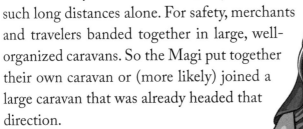

Many Bible people made long journeys. They were carried by camels, rode donkeys, and walked on foot. Let's meet some of these fascinating travelers.

1. Cain was the Bible's first traveler. He left Eden and walked east to
_____.
   a) China
   b) Canaan
   c) Burma
   d) Nod

2. Confused people speaking new languages left _____ and went all over the earth.
   a) Babylon
   b) Babel
   c) Barbados
   d) Bilbo

3. How old was Abram when he left Haran and journeyed south into Canaan?
   a) forty
   b) seventy-five
   c) one hundred
   d) two hundred

4. Abraham sent his servant far to the north with ten camels to find
_____.
   a) the Holy Grail
   b) the Fountain of Youth
   c) a bride for his son
   d) Santa Claus

5. Why did Jacob quickly leave home and walk 450 miles to the city of Haran?
   a) to get some exercise
   b) to find a job as a shepherd
   c) to attend his uncle's wedding
   d) to flee from his brother

6. What animal was the preferred "vehicle" for the armies of Midian when Gideon served as judge of Israel?
   a) mule
   b) horse
   c) camel
   d) elephant

7. This prince of Egypt ran away through the desert to the land of Midian.
   a) Ramses
   b) Moses
   c) Joseph
   d) Charlton Heston

8. Balaam rode a donkey from Pethor (near the Euphrates River) to _____.
   a) Germany
   b) Persia
   c) Moab
   d) the Nile River

9. It took Ezra and a group of Jews four months to walk to Jerusalem. What was the first thing they did when they arrived?

    a) bathed in the Jordan River

    b) rested for three days

    c) danced around the temple

    d) complained about the manna

10. When Mary was pregnant, she and Joseph traveled from _____ to Bethlehem.

    a) Jerusalem

    b) Nazareth

    c) Bethany

    d) Sea World

11. When God told Joseph to take Mary and Jesus to Egypt, how soon did Joseph go?

    a) that same night

    b) first thing the next morning

    c) after he got home from work

    d) when it was convenient

12. Many Jews attended the feast of Pentecost in Jerusalem. Where did they come from?

    a) only Judea

    b) only Judea and Parthia

    c) only Parthia

    d) Judea and many nations

ANSWERS

1. d) Nod (Genesis 4:16)
2. b) Babel (Genesis 11:8–9)
3. b) seventy-five (Genesis 12:4–5)
4. c) a bride for his son (Genesis 24:3–10)
5. d) to flee from his brother (Genesis 27:41–44)
6. c) camel (Judges 6:1–14)
7. b) Moses (Exodus 2:11–15)
8. c) Moab (Numbers 22:4–6, 21, 36)
9. b) rested for three days (Ezra 7:6–9; 8:32)
10. b) Nazareth (Luke 2:4–5)
11. a) that same night (Matthew 2:13–14 NLT)
12. d) Judea and many nations (Acts 2:1–11)

As you've seen from these questions and answers, God's people sometimes had to make long overland journeys. But such trips were usually once-in-a-lifetime experiences. Normally, people stayed put and pretty much lived their entire lives in one place. The only folks who trekked to far-off locations and back again fairly often were merchants—and the camel drivers who worked for them. They did that because it was their job.

Some caravans used donkeys to transport goods. Donkeys were smaller than camels, but they were very strong and could carry quite a bit. But the all-time champions for carrying heavy loads of valuable cargo long distances were camels, and they could travel twenty-five miles in one day. Camels are still called "ships of the desert."

7

MERCHANTS AND TRADE ROUTES

When Jesus was born, merchants were constantly traveling all over the Roman Empire—and to and from faraway countries. Every year, hundreds of tons of rare goods were transported from distant eastern lands, including spices and perfumes from India and silk from China. The Wise Men may have traveled with such a caravan as they journeyed to Judea.

Caravans didn't just pick any path either. Whenever they could, they stuck to well-traveled roads. They wanted to take the safest, shortest route possible.

From beginning to end, from Genesis to Revelation, the Bible talks about merchants transporting goods long distances in order to earn a profit. In fact, Jesus Himself told stories about merchants and traders. How well do you know these Bible stories? Let's find out.

1. A caravan of _____, heading to Egypt, took Joseph there and sold him as a slave.
   a) Joseph's brothers
   b) Canaanites
   c) Ishmaelites
   d) Esau's men

2. When the queen of Sheba visited Solomon, what did she bring on her camels?
   a) only food for her journey
   b) spices, gold, and precious stones
   c) chests full of precious pearls
   d) five tons of chocolate

3. What unusual things did King Solomon's merchant ships bring him every three years?
   a) apes and monkeys
   b) jars of honey and peanut butter
   c) blocks of ice
   d) pirate treasure

4. What fast four-legged animals did Solomon's merchants import from Egypt?
   a) kangaroos
   b) frogs
   c) ostriches
   d) horses

5. What did Solomon say "is like the merchant ships," bringing "food from afar"?

   a) a fast camel
   b) a sturdy donkey
   c) a virtuous wife
   d) a merchant ship

6. Nehemiah said, "Once or twice the merchants and sellers of all kinds of goods spent the _____ outside Jerusalem."

   a) gold coins
   b) silver coins
   c) copper coins
   d) night

7. Jesus said that the kingdom of heaven is like a merchant seeking _____.

   a) birds of paradise
   b) beautiful pearls
   c) golden ponies
   d) sugar and spice

8. Jesus told a parable about a man who gave his servants some money before he went away. What did his *wise* servants do?

   a) hid the money in a hole
   b) put it in a bank to earn interest
   c) bought a football team
   d) traded with it and earned more money

9. Nard was an expensive perfume from India. What did Mary do with a whole jar of nard?

   a) wore it on special events

   b) poured it on Jesus' head and feet

   c) sold it and gave the money to the poor

   d) kept it in a closet and never used it

10. Why was James upset when merchants said that they'd go to another city to "buy and sell, and make a profit"?

   a) It's wrong to buy and sell.

   b) It's wrong to make a profit.

   c) It's wrong to go to another city.

   d) They were boasting.

11. This cloth (from China) was sold in the markets of Babylon the Great.

   a) wool

   b) cotton

   c) silk

   d) nylon

12. When Babylon the Great burns, why will all the earth's merchants weep?

   a) No one buys their merchandise anymore.

   b) The smoke gets in their eyes.

   c) The fire is so very, very hot.

   d) The firecracker factory catches fire.

ANSWERS

1. c) Ishmaelites (Genesis 37:25–28 NKJV)
2. b) spices, gold, and precious stones (1 Kings 10:1–2)
3. a) apes and monkeys (1 Kings 10:22 NKJV)
4. d) horses (1 Kings 10:28)
5. c) a virtuous wife (Proverbs 31:10, 14 NKJV)
6. d) night (Nehemiah 13:20 NIV)
7. b) beautiful pearls (Matthew 13:45 NKJV)
8. d) traded with it and earned more money (Matthew 25:14–28)
9. b) poured it on Jesus' head and feet (Mark 14:3; John 12:1–8 NIV)
10. d) They were boasting. (James 4:13–17 NKJV)
11. c) silk (Revelation 18:10–12)
12. a) No one buys their merchandise anymore. (Revelation 18:10–11)

It took a lot of money and effort to organize a caravan, and merchants often traveled such long distances that they tried to make the trips *really* worthwhile. (Sometimes they had hundreds of camels in a long "camel train.") Camel drivers knew exactly how much the average camel could carry day after day—a little over 400 pounds, to be exact—so they made sure that every pound was something that could be sold for great profit.

For the merchants and camel drivers, such trips were strictly business and probably pretty boring much of the time. Not so for the three Wise Men! They were on a spiritual pilgrimage to find the King of the Jews, the Lord of the World. For sure they had to count the cost of going on such a trip—and there was a high price tag—but it was pure joy that motivated them!

8

EATING AND DRINKING

Did you ever wonder what the Wise Men *ate* on their journey or where they got their food? Some people think they crossed sand dunes the entire way, so they had to carry all their food with them on camels. After all, figs, dates, and nuts keep well on long journeys. Yes, they needed to bring food and grain for their camels when crossing the desert, but much of their way went past towns, fields, and gardens, so they bought vegetables, fruits, meat, and fresh bread from local markets. When they stopped to rest, they cooked hot stews.

And as long as they were traveling along rivers like the Euphrates, their camels never went thirsty. And the Magi would have drunk from wells. The Bible has a lot to say about the foods people ate and tells several stories about them at wells. Let's have a look.

1. When three travelers came to his camp, Abraham fed them bread, meat, and _____.
   a) curds and milk
   b) beans and wine
   c) dates and water
   d) gingerbread men

2. After Rebecca had watered all ten of Eliezar's camels, what did she offer them?
   a) more water
   b) milk powder
   c) straw and fodder
   d) wood shavings

3. To whom did a wealthy woman named Abigail give two hundred loaves of bread?
   a) a group of prophets
   b) a flock of ravens
   c) the Salvation Army
   d) David and his men

4. What exactly did King Solomon grow in his royal garden?
   a) very pretty flowers
   b) fruit and spices
   c) vegetables and fruits
   d) vegetables only

5. When King Jeroboam's wife visited the prophet Ahijah, what gifts did she give?

    a) ten silver coins and a robe

    b) two lambs and one dove

    c) bread, cakes, and honey

    d) five used video games

6. What did a well-meaning prophet unwisely throw into Elisha's stew pot?

    a) way, way too much salt

    b) superhot chili peppers

    c) pork sausages

    d) poisonous vegetables

7. When Nehemiah was governor, how many people regularly ate at his table?

    a) 11

    b) 37

    c) 150

    d) 750

8. While Jesus was resting by the well of Sychar, where were His disciples?

    a) cooking lunch nearby

    b) resting in the shade of a tree

    c) drawing water from the well

    d) in the town, buying food

9. What did Jesus use to miraculously feed a crowd of five thousand people?

    a) two thousand loaves of bread

    b) five loaves and two fish

    c) manna and quail

    d) eight granola bars

10. A woman told Jesus that "_____ eat the crumbs which fall from their masters' table."

    a) fat mice

    b) little dogs

    c) hungry hamsters

    d) talking parrots

11. What did Jesus' disciples give Him to eat the day He rose from the dead?

    a) a piece of broiled fish

    b) some grapes

    c) some bread with butter

    d) some cheese

12. What did Jesus say He'd do if anyone heard Him knocking and opened the door?

    a) give them a message

    b) come in and rest awhile

    c) enter and eat with them

    d) let Thorin and his dwarves in

ANSWERS

1. a) curds and milk (Genesis 18:6–8 NIV)
2. c) straw and fodder (Genesis 24:22–25)
3. d) David and his men (1 Samuel 25:18–20, 35)
4. b) fruit and spices (Song of Songs 4:13–14)
5. c) bread, cakes, and honey (1 Kings 14:1–3)
6. d) poisonous vegetables (2 Kings 4:38–41)
7. c) 150 (Nehemiah 5:17)
8. d) in the town, buying food (John 4:4–8)
9. b) five loaves and two fish (Matthew 14:13–21)
10. b) little dogs (Matthew 15:27 NKJV)
11. a) a piece of broiled fish (Luke 24:36–43)
12. c) enter and eat with them (Revelation 3:20)

How did you do on these questions about eating and drinking in Bible times? Did you find most of them fairly easy, or were some a little tricky? Or did you find yourself wondering at times, "How on earth am I expected to know the answer to *that* question?" Simple. By rereading all those Bible-story books lying around your house.

Actually, you should be ready to graduate from Bible-story books and jump right into reading the Bible itself. If you've never read the amazing stories in the book of Genesis, you're really missing out! If you've never read the Gospels about Jesus, or the book of Acts in the New Testament, you're lacking some basic truths. Why not begin reading your Bible today?

9

BANDITS AND RAIDERS

In the ancient world, nations were often at war with each other, and when wars broke out, they pretty much brought trade to a halt. Merchants couldn't get their camels through the borders if armies were fighting there. Fortunately, when the Wise Men traveled to Judea, the *Pax Romana* (Roman Peace) was in effect, and the trade routes were busy with caravans.

However, the Magi still faced danger from groups of bandits and desert raiders. Robbers especially targeted caravans because they knew that they were carrying very costly merchandise. That's why large caravans had armed guards riding with them, keeping a sharp lookout. Plus, all able-bodied men carried weapons like swords, spears, bows, and daggers. They hoped that they wouldn't have to fight, but they were prepared, just in case.

1. In Abraham's day, foreign armies _____ Sodom and other cities of Canaan.
  a) paid a friendly visit to
  b) raided and plundered
  c) just passed through
  d) bombed

2. What did the foreign armies do that made Abraham and his men attack them?
  a) They robbed Abraham's caravan.
  b) They stole Abraham's sheep.
  c) They kidnapped Abraham's wife.
  d) They took Abraham's nephew.

3. The Sabaeans, a desert tribe, raided Job's land and took his _____ away.
  a) oxen and donkeys
  b) olives and figs
  c) sons and daughters
  d) gravel truck

4. In Gideon's day, countless Midianite raiders, who were _____, invaded Israel.
  a) as fast as hornets
  b) as numerous as locusts
  c) as small as ants
  d) as colorful as butterflies

5. Jephthah had a band of rough men in the land of Tob. How were they like Vikings?

    a) They spoke Swedish.

    b) They didn't mind cold winters.

    c) They sailed in long ships.

    d) They went out raiding.

6. While David and his men were away, the Amalekites raided their town, _____.

    a) Mount Gerizim

    b) Bethlehem

    c) Ziklag

    d) Manhattan

7. Arabians and Philistines invaded and took everything from King Jehoram's _____.

    a) palace

    b) toy factory

    c) supermarkets

    d) bank machines

8. Ezra led a group of Jews on a dangerous journey for four months without _____.

    a) food or water

    b) stopping to rest

    c) soldiers to guard them

    d) knowing where they were going

9. In the story of the Good Samaritan, a man was attacked by bandits on _____.
   a) the interstate highway
   b) Jerusalem's main street
   c) the road to Jericho
   d) the Mount of Olives

10. Jesus said thieves come to steal, kill, and destroy, but He came so we might _____.
   a) not be thieves
   b) have wisdom
   c) become rich
   d) have life

11. Paul wrote that _____ will happen like a "thief in the night."
   a) Christmas Day
   b) the day of the Lord
   c) a bank robbery
   d) a contest

12. Paul said that he had traveled a lot and had often been in danger from _____.
   a) bandits
   b) Roman soldiers
   c) cattle stampedes
   d) reindeer

ANSWERS

1. b) raided and plundered (Genesis 14:5–11)
2. d) they took Abraham's nephew (Genesis 14:12–14)
3. a) oxen and donkeys (Job 1:1, 14–15)
4. b) as numerous as locusts (Judges 6:1–5 NKJV)
5. d) they went out raiding (Judges 11:3 NKJV)
6. c) Ziklag (1 Samuel 30:1)
7. a) palace (2 Chronicles 21:16–17)
8. c) soldiers to guard them (Ezra 7:8–9; 8:21–23, 31–32)
9. c) the road to Jericho (Luke 10:30)
10. d) have life (John 10:10)
11. b) the day of the Lord (1 Thessalonians 5:2)
12. a) bandits (2 Corinthians 11:26 NIV)

How did you do in this round of questions? Were they harder or easier than the last ones? Did you have to guess the answers to some questions—and did you guess correctly? Most importantly, did you gain any new gems of knowledge? There are lots of treasures in the Bible, if you want them. They're yours for the taking!

The thing that bandits, thieves, robbers, and raiders all have in common, however, is that they take treasure that *doesn't* belong to them. This breaks one of the Ten Commandments in which God says, "Thou shalt not steal" (Exodus 20:15 KJV). And in the New Testament Paul writes, "If you are a thief, quit stealing. Instead, use your hands for good hard work, and then give generously to others in need" (Ephesians 4:28 NLT).

10

SLEEPING AND BEDS

The Wise Men didn't ride nonstop for a couple of months all the way to Judea. They had to stop and rest. Their camels needed to get some sleep too. Camels can kneel down pretty much anywhere on the ground and doze—and often the Magi had to bed down on the ground as well. Not only was that a bit uncomfortable, but sleeping outside left them open to raiders' attacks.

That's why, whenever they could, the Wise Men slept in a caravansary, a lodging place for travelers, built along the caravan routes. These were inns with a large courtyard for camels and other animals. Tall, thick walls kept out robbers. There, in the safety of the caravansary, travelers enjoyed delicious meals and got a good night's sleep—all for a reasonable price.

Now let's see where *other* people slept in Bible times.

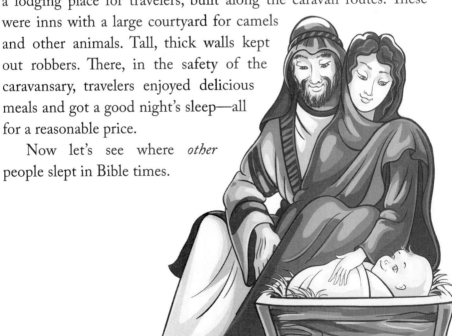

1. Abraham, Isaac, and Jacob lived in and slept in _____ most of their lives.
   a) houses
   b) palaces
   c) tents
   d) pajamas

2. Where did two angels say they'd sleep, when they first arrived in Sodom?
   a) in an inn
   b) in Lot's house
   c) in the city square
   d) in the clouds

3. _____ slept on the ground with a stone for a pillow.
   a) Jacob
   b) Samson
   c) Goliath
   d) Fred Flintstone

4. Jacob did this job for twenty years, and he missed a lot of sleep because of it.
   a) baking bread
   b) guarding a palace
   c) teaching school
   d) shepherding

5. Moses warned the Egyptians that many, many Nile River frogs would _____.
  a) croak all night
  b) cover their beds
  c) eat their grain
  d) give them warts

6. Why, when Saul sent men to get David, did Michal say David was sick in bed?
  a) He really was sick.
  b) He didn't want to fight Goliath.
  c) He didn't want to play the harp.
  d) Saul wanted to kill him.

7. When Saul hunted him, David hid out and slept in the _____ of Adullum.
  a) house
  b) cave
  c) town
  d) garden

8. Which king lay on his bed and pouted when he couldn't get what he wanted?
  a) Ahab
  b) Saul
  c) David
  d) Herod

9. _____ slept on a ship during a violent storm.

a) Peter

b) Popeye

c) Jonah

d) Esau

10. What did Princess Jehoshabeath cleverly hide in a palace bedroom?

a) her golden necklace

b) baby Joash and his nanny

c) her secret diary

d) herself

11. In Jesus' parable, a man didn't want to get out of bed at midnight and _____.

a) lock the door

b) give someone bread

c) change a diaper

d) get a snack

12. In _____ Jesus' disciples fell asleep instead of staying awake to pray.

a) the upper room

b) Mary and Martha's house

c) the wilderness

d) the Garden of Gethsemane

ANSWERS

1. c) tents (Hebrews 11:8–9 NKJV)
2. c) in the city square (Genesis 19:1–2)
3. a) Jacob (Genesis 28:10–11)
4. d) shepherding (Genesis 31:38–40)
5. b) cover their beds (Exodus 8:3)
6. d) Saul wanted to kill him (1 Samuel 19:11–15)
7. b) cave (1 Samuel 22:1)
8. a) Ahab (1 Kings 21:4)
9. c) Jonah (Jonah 1:4–6)
10. b) baby Joash and his nanny (2 Chronicles 22:11)
11. b) give someone bread (Luke 11:5–8)
12. d) the Garden of Gethsemane (Matthew 26:36–43)

How did you do with these questions? Did you remember the answers, or were you half asleep in Sunday school when those stories were told? Or are you quite certain that you never heard some of them before? If that's the case, make sure to look up the Bible references and read the stories for yourself. You have to admit, some of them sound downright interesting. And they definitely are!

Speaking of interesting facts, here's a bonus question: Which prophet of God once wished that he had his own caravansary? (a) Moses, (b) Elijah, (c) Jeremiah, or (d) Ezekiel? The answer is (c) Jeremiah. He wrote: "Oh, that I had in the desert a lodging place for travelers" (Jeremiah 9:2 NIV).

THOSE WISE MEN

Find the following **bold-face** words in the puzzle grid above. If words are **bold and underlined**, they'll be together in the puzzle!

After **Jesus** was born in **Bethlehem** in **Judea**, during the time of <u>**King Herod**</u>, **Magi** from the **east** came to **Jerusalem** and asked, "Where is the one who has been **born** king of the **Jews**? We saw <u>**his star**</u> when <u>**it rose**</u> and have come to **worship** him."
MATTHEW 2:1–2 NIV

```
K  P  I  H  S  R  O  W  J  E
B  J  E  R  U  S  A  L  E  M
L  E  A  S  T  D  N  O  W  I
M  S  T  N  H  A  E  B  S  T
E  U  E  H  I  S  S  T  A  R
C  S  U  O  L  T  B  J  T  O
K  I  N  G  H  E  R  O  D  S
Z  E  A  R  D  S  H  Y  R  E
L  O  C  H  J  U  D  E  A  N
I  T  N  T  O  I  G  A  M  L
```

AN UNHAPPY KING

Read the whole story in Matthew 2:1–23!

Across

3. He was king when Jesus was born (2:1)
5. Where the king sent the Wise Men (2:8)
7. Top age of the boys the king ordered killed (2:16)

Down

1. What the king said he would do when he saw baby Jesus (2:8)
2. The prophet who predicted the king's angry reaction (2:17)
4. How God warned Joseph of the king's plans (2:13)
6. Where Joseph, Mary, and baby Jesus escaped to (2:14)

11

THE ROMANS

If their caravan followed the main, most-traveled trade route—which it most likely did—the Wise Men would have trekked west then headed north up the Euphrates River. Until this time, they'd been traveling through the Parthian Empire. But then they came to the caravan city of Dura-Europus. From here they rode their camels across a shallow ford in the river and entered the Roman Empire.

The Roman Empire covered a vast territory from the Euphrates River in the east to Spain in the far west. At this time, the Romans were at peace with the Parthians, so they stopped the Wise Men's caravan just long enough to see what merchandise they were carrying and to make them pay taxes on it.

The Romans were an amazing people and had a great civilization. The Bible has a lot to say about them. Let's have a look now.

1. Who was caesar (emperor) of the Romans when Jesus was born?
   a) Claudius
   b) Nero
   c) Hadrian
   d) Augustus

2. John the Baptist said that Roman soldiers should be content with _____.
   a) their food
   b) their wages
   c) their old sandals
   d) their commanders

3. What did a kind Roman centurion (officer) in Capernaum build for the Jews?
   a) a prison
   b) a swimming pool
   c) a synagogue
   d) a corner store

4. What did that same Roman centurion in Capernaum ask Jesus?
   a) how to be saved
   b) whether he should pay taxes
   c) directions to Jerusalem
   d) to heal his servant

5. Jesus once showed the Pharisees a coin. Whose image was stamped on that coin?
   a) Caesar's
   b) Herod's
   c) Pilate's
   d) Abraham Lincoln's

6. Pilate, the Roman governor, wanted to free Jesus because he knew Jesus was _____.
   a) a troublemaker
   b) innocent
   c) the Messiah
   d) a carpenter

7. Which Roman centurion became a Christian when Peter told him about Jesus?
   a) Julius
   b) Maximilian
   c) Romanus
   d) Cornelius

8. Which of Jesus' apostles was a Roman citizen from his birth?
   a) Peter
   b) Andrew
   c) Bartholomew
   d) Paul

9. Why did Claudius Lysias send Paul to the Roman governor Felix?
   a) to execute him
   b) to protect him
   c) as a dinner guest
   d) to bring him a gift

10. Julius, a Roman officer, knew Paul very well because they _____ together.
   a) spent winter on an island
   b) went golfing on weekends
   c) attended the same church
   d) worked in the same factory

11. God promised Paul that he would arrive safely in Rome and _____.
   a) visit Julius's family
   b) see the tourist sites
   c) stand before Caesar
   d) speak with the pope

12. Paul described a Roman soldier's armor to show us what _____ was like.
   a) a Roman soldier
   b) the armor of God
   c) ancient armor
   d) everyday clothing

ANSWERS

1. d) Augustus (Luke 2:1–7)
2. b) their wages (Luke 3:14)
3. c) a synagogue (Luke 7:1–5)
4. d) to heal his servant (Matthew 8:5–7)
5. a) Caesar's (Matthew 22:15–22)
6. b) innocent (Luke 23:13–22)
7. d) Cornelius (Acts 10:24, 44–48)
8. d) Paul (Acts 22:25–28)
9. b) to protect him (Acts 23:23–33)
10. a) spent winter on an island (Acts 27:1; 28:1, 11)
11. c) stand before Caesar (Acts 27:23–24)
12. b) the armor of God (Ephesians 6:11–17)

For hundreds of years, the Roman army was one of the greatest military forces on earth, and they conquered a vast empire from Britain in the west to the Euphrates River in the east. Roman soldiers also served as police officers within the Empire. Paul urged Christians to obey Roman law and to respect those who enforced it. He wrote, "Everyone must submit to governing authorities. For all authority comes from God, and those in positions of authority have been placed there by God" (Romans 13:1 NLT).

Roman soldiers often protected Paul from danger. Unfortunately, later some of the foolish emperors like Nero ordered the government to persecute Christians. However, Christians stood firm and refused to give up their faith, and in the end Christianity became the official religion of the entire Empire.

12

WILD ANIMALS

Once they left the Euphrates River behind, the Wise Men's caravan passed few villages and farms. Soon they were crossing barren lands where wild animals lived. As the Magi hurried west across the desert to the oasis city of Palmyra, they probably prayed that they wouldn't be attacked by lions or leopards. They could hear big cats roaring in the distance and see their glowing eyeballs in the darkness. And the insane cries of hyenas and jackals sent chills up their spines.

There were other, smaller dangers to watch out for in the desert—such as scorpions and serpents. And hideous vultures circled overhead, waiting for something to die so they could swoop down and pick the carcass clean. Wild animals were a constant threat throughout Bible times. How much do you know about these creatures?

1. Poor Jacob thought that some wild beast had killed and eaten his
_____.
   a) favorite lamb
   b) pet dog
   c) son Joseph
   d) cat

2. In Bible times, _____ ran around in the wilderness near Job's
land.
   a) penguins
   b) dodos
   c) turkeys
   d) ostriches

3. The children of Israel were in danger from _____ in the desert.
   a) stingrays
   b) scorpions
   c) rattlesnakes
   d) wild donkeys

4. Moses made _____ that cured people who had been bitten by
snakes.
   a) a brass (or bronze) snake
   b) an antivenom serum
   c) a hospital
   d) a Band-Aid

5. God used _____ to help drive the Canaanites out of Canaan.
   a) ants
   b) locusts
   c) hornets
   d) cockroaches

6. Samson found _____ full of honey.
   a) a dog
   b) a lion
   c) a donkey
   d) Winnie the Pooh

7. David killed _____ when they attacked his sheep.
   a) a lion and a hyena
   b) a wolf and a jackal
   c) a leopard and a bear
   d) a bear and a lion

8. A disobedient prophet was _____ when a lion attacked and killed him.
   a) riding his donkey
   b) gambling
   c) talking to the king
   d) running from Nineveh

9. Jeremiah asked if _____ could change its spots.
   a) a giraffe
   b) a cheetah
   c) a leopard
   d) a Dalmatian

10. Isaiah said _____ would live in Babylon's ruins.
   a) tigers and elephants
   b) hyenas and jackals
   c) skunks and rabbits
   d) alligators and crocodiles

11. When talking about the Good Shepherd, Jesus said _____ attacked sheep.
   a) a lion
   b) a bear
   c) a wolf
   d) a snake

12. Isaiah wrote that one day tame goats would _____ leopards.
   a) run away from
   b) lie down beside
   c) be in circus acts with
   d) fight and conquer

ANSWERS

1. c) son Joseph (Genesis 37:31–33)
2. d) ostriches (Job 39:13–18)
3. b) scorpions (Deuteronomy 8:15)
4. a) a brass (or bronze) snake (Numbers 21:4–9 NIV)
5. c) hornets (Exodus 23:28; Joshua 24:12)
6. b) a lion (Judges 14:5–8)
7. d) a bear and a lion (1 Samuel 17:34–37)
8. a) riding his donkey (1 Kings 13:20–24)
9. c) a leopard (Jeremiah 13:23)
10. b) hyenas and jackals (Isaiah 13:19–22 NIV)
11. c) a wolf (John 10:11–15)
12. b) lie down beside (Isaiah 11:6)

Did you imagine that the Bible contained so many stories and so much information about wild animals? And that's only *some* of it! God's Word also talks about prides of lions killing foreigners because they didn't worship the Lord (2 Kings 17:24–25), and leopards lurking outside city gates (Jeremiah 5:6). And of course, there's the classic story of Daniel spending one very *looong* night in a den with hungry lions (Daniel 6). And let's not forget Noah and his floating zoo.

When we travel today, we're not usually concerned about savage beasts attacking us. There aren't a lot of lions and leopards left in the world. They're now extinct in many countries. But back when the Wise Men were on the road to see baby Jesus, wild animals were a very real concern.

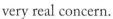

13

ROBES AND TURBANS

Many Christmas cards show the three Wise Men dressed in rich robes and wearing crowns or bright turbans as they pause on a hill to look at the Star. But even if they *were* kings, that's not how they would have dressed while traveling down dusty roads or across sandy, windy deserts. They would have worn travel clothing all the way there and only put on their best robes before seeing King Herod and before visiting Jesus.

In other words, they dressed like regular travelers most of the time. Well then, what does the Bible say about how people dressed in those days? You've probably seen enough pictures in Bible storybooks to know that most folks back then wore robes and sandals. But there's more to it than that. Are you ready for the next set of questions? Great! Then let's begin.

1. Israel (Jacob) gave Joseph _____.
   a) a new video game
   b) a pony
   c) a bag of shekels
   d) a coat of many colors

2. Israelites wore a thick outer cloak to keep warm. They also used their cloaks for _____.
   a) Klingon cloaking devices
   b) turbans
   c) blankets to sleep in
   d) kites

3. While the elders of Bethlehem watched, a man gave Boaz _____.
   a) a brand-new turban
   b) a pair of sandals
   c) one sandal
   d) a pair of socks

4. While Saul wasn't looking, David _____ Saul's robe.
   a) cut a piece off
   b) hand washed
   c) hung up
   d) stored grain in

5. Jesus described _____ as being more magnificent than King Solomon's royal robes.
   a) the queen of Sheba's robes
   b) lilies of the field
   c) a rainbow
   d) a sunset

6. Proud Jewish women wore _____.
   a) headbands and sweaters
   b) golden skirts
   c) new designer jeans
   d) headbands and capes

7. Jeremiah bought a brand-new sash (cloth belt) and _____.
   a) hid it in a hole in a rock
   b) wore it proudly
   c) gave it to his cousin
   d) accidentally ripped it

8. God said, "Your _____ shall be on your heads and your sandals on your feet."
   a) water pots
   b) turbans
   c) straw hats
   d) stocking caps

9. John the Baptist's clothing was made out of _____.
   a) white linen
   b) badger skins
   c) camel's hair
   d) silk

10. When Jesus was arrested, a young man followed Him, wearing only _____.
    a) an undergarment
    b) a cloak
    c) swimming trunks
    d) a linen cloth

11. The Roman soldiers decided which of them got Jesus' clothing by _____.
    a) flipping a coin
    b) arm wrestling
    c) throwing dice
    d) each picking something

12. Peter took off his _____ when he was fishing in a boat.
    a) raincoat
    b) outer garment
    c) leather gloves
    d) wristwatch

ANSWERS

1. d) a coat of many colors (Genesis 37:3–4)
2. c) blankets to sleep in (Exodus 22:26–27)
3. c) one sandal (Ruth 4:1–8)
4. a) cut a piece off (1 Samuel 24:1–4)
5. b) lilies of the field (Matthew 6:28–29 NKJV)
6. d) headbands and capes (Isaiah 3:16–23 NIV)
7. a) hid it in a hole in a rock (Jeremiah 13:1–11)
8. b) turbans (Ezekiel 24:23 NKJV)
9. c) camel's hair (Matthew 3:4)
10. d) a linen cloth (Mark 14:51–52)
11. c) throwing dice (Matthew 27:35 NLT)
12. b) outer garment (John 21:7 NIV)

The Bible gives a clear description of what people looked like after they had traveled for many hundreds of miles. God had told the Israelites not to make a peace treaty with the nearby Canaanite cities, but the Canaanites of Gibeon really wanted to avoid war, so they sent some men who pretended to be ambassadors from a far country. When they arrived in the Israelite camp, their donkeys were carrying beaten-up wineskins and worn food sacks with old, moldy bread. The men's clothing was old and dusty, and their sandals were old and patched (see Joshua 9:3–15).

When a caravan pulled into town after months on the road, that's pretty much what the merchants and travelers looked like. That is, until they opened their travel bags, pulled out fresh, clean robes, and dressed up to do business.

14

PALACES AND HOMES

When the Wise Men arrived at Jerusalem, they probably first stopped at a caravansary outside the city walls. There they washed, dressed in their best, and prepared to meet King Herod. Then, bearing their gifts, together with their servants they proceeded to his palace. Herod was, after all, king of Judea, so they expected to find the newborn King of the Jews there.

Herod's palace was situated in the highest part of the city of Jerusalem. It had many chambers and large bedrooms filled with fine furniture and vessels of gold and silver. Herod lived in decadent luxury, and everything his heart desired was found in his palatial estate. Most of the people he ruled over didn't live quite as large. Let's look at the high and mighty homes of other kings, as well as the lowly, humble homes of average Israelites.

1. What poured into Pharaoh's great palace in Moses' day?
   a) the Nile River
   b) an entire jug of olive oil
   c) swarms of flies
   d) an overflowing bathtub

2. What material did King Hiram of Tyre send to David to build a palace out of?
   a) huge stone blocks
   b) sheets of plywood
   c) ten tons of nails
   d) cedar logs

3. How long did it take Solomon to build his new palace?
   a) three months
   b) seven years
   c) thirteen years
   d) he never finished it

4. Solomon also built a palace for whom?
   a) his oldest son
   b) Pharaoh's daughter
   c) his pet lions
   d) his favorite musician

5. What was King Zimri's final act as king of Israel?
   a) He built a new palace.
   b) He covered the palace with gold.
   c) He filled the palace with cats.
   d) He burned down the palace.

6. King Ahab covered the walls of his palace with _____.
   a) ivory decorations
   b) leopard skins
   c) wood carvings
   d) gems

7. A poor widow told Elisha that she had
   _____ in her home.
   a) expensive furniture
   b) a new Persian rug
   c) nothing but a jar of oil
   d) an extra room for him

8. King Nebuchadnezzar was
   _____ when he lost his mind.
   a) in the royal garden
   b) on the roof
   c) in the throne room
   d) in his bedchamber

9. What change did God tell Ezekiel to make to his house in Babylon?
    a) add a bedroom
    b) put in glass windows
    c) dig a hole in his wall
    d) move it to Israel

10. Queen Vashti gave a banquet for _____ in King Xerxes's royal palace.
    a) the king and Haman
    b) Mordecai
    c) women
    d) her mother-in-law

11. Whom did Jesus say lived in palaces? People who _____.
    a) can afford to
    b) are movie stars
    c) are politicians
    d) wear expensive clothes

12. How did some men get a sick friend inside a house so Jesus could heal him?
    a) through the door
    b) through a side window
    c) through a hole in the roof
    d) down the chimney

ANSWERS

1. c) swarms of flies (Exodus 8:24 NIV)
2. d) cedar logs (1 Chronicles 14:1 NIV)
3. c) thirteen years (1 Kings 7:1)
4. b) Pharaoh's daughter (1 Kings 7:8)
5. d) He burned down the palace. (1 Kings 16:15–18)
6. a) ivory decorations (1 Kings 22:39)
7. c) nothing but a jar of oil (2 Kings 4:1–2)
8. b) on the roof (Daniel 4:29–34 NIV)
9. c) dig a hole in his wall (Ezekiel 12:1–7)
10. c) women (Esther 1:9)
11. d) wear expensive clothes (Luke 7:25)
12. c) through a hole in the roof (Mark 2:1–5)

There was quite a difference between the palaces that kings resided in and the mud-brick homes of the poor Israelites. Yet as Jesus pointed out, riches didn't matter. The Jews weren't flocking to visit King Herod, dressed in expensive clothes, living in his luxurious palace. Instead, they were going out into the desert to listen to a homeless man named John the Baptist. Why? Because John was preaching the Word of God.

Jesus Himself, although He was the King of the Jews, was born like the poorest of the poor, in a stable. And when He grew up, Jesus didn't own even a mud-brick home. He said, "Foxes have dens and birds have nests, but the Son of Man has no place to lay his head" (Matthew 8:20 NIV). Yet Jesus and John had the greatest riches in the world—eternal life. Do you?

15

SCRIBES AND SECRETARIES

When the Wise Men met King Herod, they asked, "Where is He who has been born King of the Jews? For we have seen His star in the East and have come to worship Him" (Matthew 2:2 NKJV). Herod was troubled. He was so jealous over his throne that he didn't trust his own sons—let alone a child born *outside* his family.

Herod knew that the Wise Men meant the Messiah (called the Christ), so he gathered the chief priests and scribes and asked them where the prophecies said the Christ would be born. The scribes were experts in the scriptures. Their job was to make copies of the Word of God. Day after day they carefully wrote it out word by word, letter by letter—so they knew better than anyone else what it said.

Now let's see how much *you* know about scribes in the Bible.

1. _____ wished his words were written in a book *and* engraved on a rock with an iron pen.
   a) Pharaoh
   b) Job
   c) Adam
   d) Cyrus the Great

2. _____ used his finger to write the Ten Commandments on stone tablets.
   a) Moses
   b) Aaron
   c) God
   d) The little Dutch boy

3. _____ was King David's counselor. He was a wise man and a scribe.
   a) Jehonathan, his uncle
   b) Jonathan, his friend
   c) Absalom, his son
   d) Methuselah

4. David wrote in a psalm, "...my _____ is the pen of a skillful writer."
   a) pen
   b) pencil
   c) wax crayon
   d) tongue

5. When a priest gave him a long-lost book, Shaphan the scribe

_____.

   a) made a copy of it

   b) read it to the king

   c) put it on a bookshelf

   d) lost it again

6. The scribe Baruch wrote down the prophecies of Jeremiah _____.

   a) with a reed on a clay tablet

   b) with ink on a scroll

   c) with a chisel on a stone

   d) with a stick in the sand

7. Ezekiel saw six men carrying battle-axes. At his side, another man had _____.

   a) a sword

   b) a dagger

   c) a fierce dog

   d) a writer's inkhorn

8. The prophet Zechariah saw an unusual scroll. What was so odd about it?

   a) It was half a mile long.

   b) It was covered with eyes.

   c) It was flying in the air.

   d) It could speak.

9. When he read the scriptures in Jerusalem, Ezra the scribe stood on
_____.

    a) a platform of wood

    b) the temple steps

    c) an elephant's back

    d) a moving oxcart

10. Scribes in Jesus' day carefully gave God tithes of tiny spices but
neglected _____.

    a) tithing their money

    b) personal hygiene

    c) justice and mercy

    d) copying the scriptures

11. After he had carefully learned all the
facts about the Gospel, Luke _____.

    a) bought his own copy

    b) dictated it to a scribe

    c) preached the Gospel in Spain

    d) wrote an orderly account

12. When an angel handed
him a scroll, John _____.

    a) thanked the angel

    b) ate it

    c) read it silently

    d) read it out loud

ANSWERS

1. b) Job (Job 19:1, 23–24)
2. c) God (Exodus 31:18)
3. a) Jehonathan, his uncle (1 Chronicles 27:32 NKJV)
4. d) tongue (Psalm 45:1 NIV)
5. b) read it to the king (2 Kings 22:8–10)
6. b) with ink on a scroll (Jeremiah 36:17–18 NIV)
7. d) a writer's inkhorn (Ezekiel 9:2)
8. c) it was flying in the air (Zechariah 5:1–2 NKJV)
9. a) a platform of wood (Nehemiah 8:1–4)
10. c) justice and mercy (Matthew 23:23 NKJV)
11. d) wrote an orderly account (Luke 1:1–4 NKJV)
12. b) ate it (Revelation 10:8–10)

Are you finding the quizzes are getting harder as you go along, or are you still able to get most of the answers right? Are you finding that half of the answers are old hat—you're already familiar with the stories—but the rest are brand-new and you're hearing them for the first time? If so, congratulations! You're adding new treasures to the old ones you already have.

Scribes were called "teachers of the law." They taught God's Word because they knew it so well. But as well as they knew it, they *kept* studying it and continued to learn new things. That's why Jesus said, "Every teacher of the law who has become a disciple in the kingdom of heaven is like the owner of a house who brings out of his storeroom new treasures as well as old" (Matthew 13:52 NIV).

16

O LITTLE TOWN OF BETHLEHEM

Those scribes really knew their stuff! When Herod asked where the King of the Jews would be born, they quoted a prophecy from the book of Micah. Now, most people have never even *read* that Old Testament book—they don't know it exists—but the scribes right away quoted Micah 5:2. They answered Herod, "In Bethlehem of Judea, for thus it is written by the prophet: 'But you, Bethlehem, in the land of Judah, are not the least among the rulers of Judah; for out of you shall come a Ruler who will shepherd My people Israel'" (Matthew 2:5–6 NKJV).

Jesus wasn't the only Bible person to come out of Bethlehem—although He was certainly the most important one. Let's take a look at some other men and women who were either born in Bethlehem or had something to do with it.

1. What is another name people used to describe the city in which Jesus was born?
   a) Ephrath
   b) Bethel
   c) Bethuel
   d) Memphis

2. _____—a wife of Jacob—died and was buried on the way to Bethlehem.
   a) Leah
   b) Rachel
   c) Zilpah
   d) Bilhah

3. Ibzan of Bethlehem led Israel seven years. What was he most famous for?
   a) his strange name
   b) his great strength
   c) playing the flute
   d) his sixty sons and daughters

4. There were *two* Bethlehems in Israel. What was David's Bethlehem often called?
   a) Zion
   b) Bethlehem in Judah
   c) northern Bethlehem
   d) southern Bethlehem

5. A Levite came from the _____ to get a concubine (wife) from Bethlehem.
   a) city of Nineveh
   b) hill country of Judah
   c) mountains of Ephraim
   d) pool of Siloam

6. Naomi and Ruth came from Moab to Bethlehem at the beginning of _____.
   a) the barley harvest
   b) the hockey season
   c) summer vacations
   d) Christmas holidays

7. What famous wealthy man from Bethlehem did Ruth marry?
   a) Ibzan
   b) Samson
   c) Boaz
   d) Solomon

8. Jesse, an old man of Bethlehem, had eight sons. Who was his most famous son?
   a) Jesse Jr.
   b) Jesse James
   c) Joseph
   d) David

9. David returned from Saul's palace to _____ at Bethlehem.
   a) get strings for his harp
   b) attend school
   c) feed his father's sheep
   d) visit his cousins

10. What Philistine giant did Elhanan of Bethlehem kill?
   a) Goliath
   b) Lahmi, Goliath's brother
   c) Ishbibenob
   d) Saph

11. What did David's three mightiest men risk their lives to get from Bethlehem?
   a) water from the well
   b) a treasure chest
   c) David's wife Michal
   d) a backpack

12. Before they headed to Egypt, _____ stopped at Geruth Kimham near Bethlehem.
   a) Joseph and Mary
   b) Johanan and the Jews
   c) Joseph's brothers
   d) Santa and his reindeer

ANSWERS

1. a) Ephrath (Genesis 35:19)
2. b) Rachel (Genesis 35:19)
3. d) his sixty sons and daughters (Judges 12:8–9)
4. b) Bethlehem in Judah (Judges 17:7; 1 Samuel 17:12 NKJV)
5. c) mountains of Ephraim (Judges 19:1 NKJV)
6. a) the barley harvest (Ruth 1:22)
7. c) Boaz (Ruth 2:1; 4:13)
8. d) David (1 Samuel 17:12)
9. c) feed his father's sheep (1 Samuel 17:15)
10. b) Lahmi, Goliath's brother (2 Samuel 21:19; 1 Chronicles 20:5)
11. a) water from the well (2 Samuel 23:14–16)
12. b) Johanan and the Jews (Jeremiah 41:16–17 NIV)

Another name for Bethlehem was Ephrath. (That's the answer to the first question. Did you get it right?) In Hebrew, *Ephrath* means "fruitful," and *Bethlehem* means "house of bread." Why such names? Well, Bethlehem was only five miles south of Jerusalem, and between them was the long Valley of Rephaim. There were huge fields of wheat and barley there, which were used to make bread—*lots* of it!

That's why such a small, insignificant hilltop town like Bethlehem could have such prosperous men like Boaz and Jesse. Which goes to show, you don't have to be big and powerful to have value.

It's interesting that Bethlehem means "house of bread," since Jesus was born there, and He tells us, "I am the bread of life. He who comes to Me shall never hunger, and he who believes in Me shall never thirst" (John 6:35 NKJV).

17

LED BY GOD

When the Wise Men left Herod's palace, it was probably late afternoon. And by the time they got back to the caravansary, the sun had set and the stars were coming out. And lo and behold! There in the sky was the *same star* once again! Since Bethlehem was only five miles to the south, they mounted their camels and headed there at once.

The star didn't just stay still. As the astonished Magi watched, it moved ahead of them, south toward Bethlehem. When they arrived a couple of hours later, the amazing star came to a stop over one of the houses. As "The First Noel" says, "O'er Bethlehem it took its rest, and there it did both stop and stay, right o'er the place where Jesus lay."

Other Bible people were also miraculously guided to specific places and specific people. Let's look at their stories now.

1. After Abraham's servant prayed, God miraculously led _____ to him.
   a) Abraham
   b) his missing donkey
   c) Rebekah
   d) Miriam

2. God showed the children of Israel the way by going before them in a _____.
   a) fiery chariot
   b) Cadillac
   c) bolt of lightning
   d) pillar of cloud

3. Samuel told _____ which way to go, and prophesied whom he'd meet on the way.
   a) Saul
   b) Absalom
   c) Jonah
   d) Thomas

4. God told David *twice* to go to this Israelite city, to save it from the Philistines.
   a) Gath
   b) Keilah
   c) Damascus
   d) Hollywood

5. How did the Holy Spirit show John the Baptist that Jesus was God's Son?
   a) He drove him into the wilderness.
   b) He led him into the temple.
   c) He descended on Jesus like a dove.
   d) He sent John an e-mail.

6. _____ led Jesus' disciples to the house where they ate a Passover meal.
   a) A man carrying a jug of water
   b) A trail of ants
   c) A talking donkey
   d) A temple guard

7. Where did an angel tell Philip to go?
   a) South America
   b) south on the Gaza Road
   c) the South Pole
   d) the North Pole

8. Where did God tell Ananias to go in Damascus? (Ananias did *not* want to go there.)
   a) Herod's palace on Main Street
   b) the king's palace in Nineveh
   c) the high priest's house
   d) Judas's house on Straight Street

9. God told Cornelius he would find the apostle Peter in this city.

    a) Joppa

    b) Rome

    c) Capernaum

    d) New York

10. God told Peter that three men had come to get him and that he should _____.

    a) run away from them

    b) hide from them

    c) pray for them

    d) go with them

11. How did God show Paul that he should go to Macedonia? Paul had a _____.

    a) map

    b) vision in the night

    c) letter of invitation

    d) soaking wet fleece

12. Who told Paul that he'd survive a shipwreck and meet Caesar in Rome?

    a) Jesus

    b) the ship's captain

    c) an angel

    d) a prophet

ANSWERS

1. c) Rebekah (Genesis 24:1–4, 10–15)
2. d) pillar of cloud (Exodus 13:18–22)
3. a) Saul (1 Samuel 9:27; 10:1–9)
4. b) Keilah (1 Samuel 23:1–5)
5. c) He descended on Jesus like a dove. (John 1:29–34)
6. a) A man carrying a jug of water (Luke 22:7–13)
7. b) south on the Gaza Road (Acts 8:26–29)
8. d) Judas's house on Straight Street (Acts 9:10–16)
9. a) Joppa (Acts 10:1–8)
10. d) go with them (Acts 10:17–20)
11. b) vision in the night (Acts 16:8–10)
12. c) an angel (Acts 27:21–26)

Archaeologists say there were only about three hundred people living in Bethlehem when Jesus was born—but there were many, many more in scattered farmhouses around the town. And babies were being born all the time. Herod thought the Wise Men would have to search from house to house for days, so he instructed them, "Go and search carefully for the young Child" (Matthew 2:8 NKJV).

Herod said he'd worship the Child once they found Him, but God knew that he intended to murder Jesus. There was no time to lose, so God guided the Magi directly to Joseph and Mary's house that same night. Wicked King Herod wasn't on speaking terms with God, so he didn't imagine that God would miraculously guide the Wise Men. But He did!

Has God ever shown you which way to go? Or has He ever helped you find something you had lost?

18

WORSHIPING JESUS

After the star stopped above the house, did the Wise Men walk up and knock on the door? Or did the noise of their arrival wake up Jesus' parents, and so Joseph opened the door to see who was there? We don't know. But one thing we know: "When they had come into the house, they saw the young Child with Mary His mother, and fell down and worshiped Him" (Matthew 2:11 NKJV).

Most Christmas cards show the Three Kings kneeling before Jesus, very dignified. But it was common in those days to throw oneself down, to fall down flat on the ground in front of royalty or divine beings. Talk about worship!

Many other people in the Bible worshiped God and His Son, Jesus Christ. Let's look at their stories now.

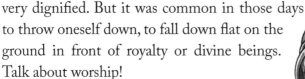

1. When disaster struck Job, he tore his robe and shaved his head. Then what did he do?
   a) He moaned, "Why me?"
   b) He sang mournful songs.
   c) He fell to the ground and worshiped.
   d) He mended his robe.

2. After Moses told the Israelites God would deliver them, they _____ and worshiped.
   a) bowed their heads
   b) cheered
   c) went to church
   d) sang hymns

3. Where did the Israelites worship when they saw God's cloud in front of His special tent?
   a) in their synagogues
   b) in the Promised Land
   c) on the street corners
   d) in their tent doorways

4. Elkanah and Hannah worshiped the Lord _____ before returning home.
   a) early in the morning
   b) with baby Samuel
   c) silently, in their hearts,
   d) with tambourines and harps

5. After King Solomon prayed, why did the Israelites bow down and worship God?

   a) Solomon told them to.

   b) They were tired of standing.

   c) God's glory filled the temple.

   d) An angel appeared.

6. In King Hezekiah's day, the Levites _____ and worshiped.

   a) burned incense

   b) closed their hymnbooks

   c) turned off the TV

   d) sang praises

7. When Nehemiah was governor, people confessed their sins and worshiped God _____.

   a) for one hour

   b) for one-fourth of the day

   c) all day long

   d) for one week nonstop

8. Who worshiped Jesus and said, "Lord, if You are willing, You can make me clean"?

   a) a pig herder

   b) the Prodigal Son

   c) a leper

   d) a fisherman

9. Why did the disciples in the boat worship Jesus, saying, "Truly You are the Son of God"?
    a) He had asked, "Who am I?"
    b) He had told a parable.
    c) He had walked on water.
    d) It was the Sabbath.

10. Why did women hold Jesus by the feet and worship Him one Sunday morning?
    a) He had told them to
    b) He had risen from the dead
    c) to keep Him from leaving
    d) they did this every Sunday

11. What did Peter say when Cornelius fell down at his feet and worshiped him?
    a) "Did you trip, Cornelius?"
    b) "Thank you very much."
    c) "Stop! You're embarrassing me."
    d) "Stand up; I myself am also a man."

12. Who exactly was standing before God's throne then fell down and worshiped Him?
    a) all the angels
    b) the twenty-four elders
    c) the four living creatures
    d) all of the above

ANSWERS

1. c) He fell to the ground and worshiped. (Job 1:13–20)
2. a) bowed their heads (Exodus 3:15–17; 4:29–31)
3. d) in their tent doorways (Exodus 33:10)
4. a) early in the morning (1 Samuel 1:19)
5. c) God's glory filled the temple. (2 Chronicles 7:1–3)
6. d) sang praises (2 Chronicles 29:30 NKJV)
7. b) for one-fourth of the day (Nehemiah 9:3)
8. c) a leper (Matthew 8:2 NKJV)
9. c) He had walked on water. (Matthew 14:23–33 NKJV)
10. b) He had risen from the dead (Matthew 28:5–9)
11. d) "Stand up; I myself am also a man." (Acts 10:24–26 NKJV)
12. d) all of the above (Revelation 7:11)

How did you do on these questions? Some of them are pretty tough, aren't they? Do you also find it tough to take a few moments to worship God? Remember, you don't need to fall flat on the ground. You don't even need to kneel—although that's often a good idea. When the cloud of God's glory appeared in their camp, the Israelites *stood* in the doorways of their tents and worshiped Him.

That goes to show that you can worship God lying down, kneeling, or simply standing—no matter *where* you are, or *what* you are doing. We often think that worship is something we do while we're singing in church. But it's an attitude in our hearts. When we focus our attention on God and realize how awesome He is, that's already worship. It doesn't matter where we are at the time (see John 4:19–24).

19

THE WISE MEN'S GIFTS

We pay a lot of attention to the Wise Men giving baby Jesus gifts of gold, frankincense, and myrrh. For many people, giving and receiving gifts is what Christmas is all about. Yes, this custom began with the Three Kings, but it's important to remember *why* they gave gifts.

The most important reason they gave the newborn King of the Jews rare, expensive gifts was to honor Him. This was a *part* of their worship: they not only knelt down before Him, but they gave Him gifts that had cost them quite a bit. It was common in those days for smaller kings to give greater kings valuable treasures (Psalm 72:8–11). This showed that they recognized that the greater king was their lord and master.

Let's look at other precious gifts that people in the Bible gave to kings and rulers—and to God and His Son.

1. What were some tasty gifts that Israel's sons brought Joseph, the governor of Egypt?
   a) camels and donkeys
   b) golden jewelry
   c) honey and almonds
   d) roasted grasshoppers

2. The Israelites gave _____ to build God's worship tent in the desert.
   a) diamonds and goat skins
   b) platinum and rope
   c) pearls and plastic
   d) earrings and badger skins

3. What did some worthless scoundrels bring Saul when he became king?
   a) slimy frogs
   b) no gifts at all
   c) chunks of coal
   d) counterfeit money

4. When the Israelite leaders gave King David gold, what did David use it for?
   a) to buy his family presents
   b) to make a golden calf
   c) to build God's temple
   d) nothing

5. Who brought Solomon valuable gifts from the land of Sheba?
   a) the king of Sheba
   b) the queen of Sheba
   c) the princes
   d) rich merchants

6. The Philistines gave Jehoshaphat gifts and silver. What did the Arabs give?
   a) 6,206 camels
   b) 1,112 golden nose rings
   c) 528 tons of cheese
   d) 7,700 rams and 7,700 goats

7. Isaiah said people of Ethiopia would bring gifts to God. How did he describe these people?
   a) tall
   b) short
   c) generous
   d) poor

8. Many nations brought presents for King Hezekiah and gifts for the Lord. Why? What had God just done?
   a) parted the Red Sea
   b) crowned David as king
   c) saved Judah from Assyria
   d) stopped the sun in the sky

9. Who gave money and gifts to Ezra and the Jews to rebuild God's temple?
    a) all their neighbors
    b) the citizens of Rome
    c) the poor Macedonians
    d) the US government

10. What very expensive gift did a sinful woman put on Jesus' feet?
    a) new designer sandals
    b) Christmas stockings
    c) perfume
    d) gold dust

11. Who did Jesus say had given more to God than any rich man?
    a) the rich women
    b) a poor widow
    c) a poor man
    d) the queen of Spain

12. Who will bring the glory and honor of the nations into the heavenly Jerusalem?
    a) kings of the earth
    b) bankers of the world
    c) foreign merchants
    d) happy children

ANSWERS

1. c) honey and almonds (Genesis 43:11, 26)
2. d) earrings and badger skins (Exodus 35:21–23 NKJV)
3. b) no gifts at all (1 Samuel 10:24–27)
4. c) to build God's temple (1 Chronicles 29:6–9)
5. b) the queen of Sheba (1 Kings 10:1–2, 10)
6. d) 7,700 rams and 7,700 goats (2 Chronicles 17:11)
7. a) tall (Isaiah 18:1, 7 NKJV)
8. c) saved Judah from the Assyrians (2 Chronicles 32:22–23 NIV)
9. a) all their neighbors (Ezra 1:5–6 NIV)
10. c) perfume (Luke 7:36–38 NIV)
11. b) a poor widow (Luke 21:1–4)
12. a) kings of the earth (Revelation 21:23–26)

The Wise Men gave Jesus expensive gifts—gold, frankincense, and myrrh—and many Christians believe that when the shepherds visited Him, they also gave Him gifts. This leaves many of us wondering what *we* should give Jesus. Christina Rossetti answered this question over one hundred years ago in "A Christmas Carol." She wrote: "What can I give Him, poor as I am? If I were a shepherd I would bring a lamb. If I were a Wise Man I would do my part; yet what I can I give Him: give my heart."

Remember, that's what the Wise Men were doing when they found Jesus, when they fell down and worshiped Him—they were giving Him their hearts. Have you looked for Jesus? Have you found Him? Give Him your heart today.

20

THE BIRTH ANNOUNCEMENT

After the Wise Men told Joseph and Mary that they'd traveled from a far eastern land to find the newborn King, they probably asked Mary and Joseph many questions. And they would have heard some amazing stories that night.

Mary would have told the Magi how, a little over a year earlier, they were living in the town of Nazareth to the north. And suddenly the angel Gabriel had appeared to her. He told Mary that the Spirit of God would cause her to get pregnant, and her baby would be the Son of God. The angel promised that God would give Jesus the throne of His ancestor, David. This meant that—as the Magi already knew—Jesus was the King of the Jews.

Now let's see how much *you* know about unusual babies and births in the Bible.

1. What Bible woman never had a mother and was never born?
   a) Mary
   b) Noah's wife
   c) Eve
   d) Rahab

2. Who had a son named Isaac even though she was too old to have babies?
   a) Hagar
   b) Elizabeth
   c) Methuselah's wife
   d) Sarah

3. Rebecca couldn't get pregnant for years. Finally, she had twin boys named _____.
   a) Larry and Bob
   b) James and John
   c) Peter and Andrew
   d) Jacob and Esau

4. What unusual thing was Jacob doing when he was born?
   a) crying very loudly
   b) holding Esau's heel
   c) sucking his thumb
   d) reciting poetry

5. Rachel called her second son Benoni. What did Jacob call him?
   a) Benoni
   b) Ben Hur
   c) Benjamin
   d) Benny

6. What did a baby named Zerah have on his wrist when he was born?
   a) a scarlet thread
   b) a lot of hair
   c) a Mickey Mouse watch
   d) a freckle

7. A Hebrew mother refused to kill her newborn son. What was his name?
   a) Jochabed
   b) Pharaoh's daughter
   c) Moses
   d) Ramses

8. An angel told Samson's parents they'd have a son. What was the angel's name?
   a) Manoah
   b) we don't know
   c) Michael
   d) Gabriel

9. This barren woman prayed to have a son. Then she had a boy named Samuel.

   a) Anna
   b) Annas
   c) Hannah
   d) Hanani

10. God told this man that he had been chosen as a prophet before he'd been born.

   a) Jeremiah
   b) Ezekiel
   c) Jonah
   d) Elijah Jr.

11. What baby was filled with the Holy Spirit even while in his mother's womb?

   a) David
   b) John the Baptist
   c) Nebuchadnezzar
   d) Cyrus

12. Which prophet prophesied that a virgin would give birth to a son?

   a) Isaiah
   b) Abraham
   c) Elisha
   d) Moses

ANSWERS

1. c) Eve (Genesis 2:21–23)
2. d) Sarah (Genesis 18:11; 21:1–3)
3. d) Jacob and Esau (Genesis 25:21–26)
4. b) holding Esau's heel (Genesis 25:26)
5. c) Benjamin (Genesis 35:16–18)
6. a) a scarlet thread (Genesis 38:27–30)
7. c) Moses (Exodus 1:22; 2:1–10)
8. b) we don't know (Judges 13:1–24)
9. c) Hannah (1 Samuel 1:9–11, 20)
10. a) Jeremiah (Jeremiah 1:1–5)
11. b) John the Baptist (Luke 1:13–15)
12. a) Isaiah (Isaiah 7:14; Matthew 1:18–23)

The Wise Men must've listened wide-eyed as Mary and Joseph told them that angels had appeared to them, telling them that Jesus was the Son of God and that He would save His people from their sins (Luke 1:32; Matthew 1:21). Clearly, the Magi had found much more than they'd set out to find! This child was not just an important Jewish king. These three weary travelers from a distant land were looking upon the Savior of the world.

After they got over their astonishment, they would have asked other questions such as: "You say that you come from another town called Nazareth? How did you end up here in Bethlehem—the very place where the scribes say the King of the Jews must be born?"

Ah! That brings us to the next part of our story!

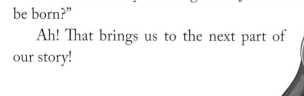

FOLLOWING A STAR

Find the following **bold-face** words in the puzzle grid above. If words are **bold and underlined**, they'll be together in the puzzle!

After they had **heard** the **king**, they went on **their way**, and the **star** they had seen when it **rose** **went ahead** of them until it **stopped** over the place where the **child** was. When they saw the star, they were **overjoyed**. On coming to the **house**, they saw the child with his **mother** **Mary**, and they bowed down and **worshiped** him.

MATTHEW 2:9–11 NIV

M L R S U M E W C H
O O E O B T A O M O
V I T C S H W R A U
E S G H Y E T S Y S
R T D I E I R H O E
J A R L O R K I N G
O R A D K W A P H O
Y W E N T A H E A D
E S H E N Y B D G L
D M O D E P P O T S

VALUABLE GIFTS

The Wise Men gave the baby Jesus three very valuable gifts. What do you know about those gifts?

Across

2. Somebody mixed myrrh with this, and offered it to Jesus while He was on the cross (Mark 15:23)
4. This wise king, an ancestor of Jesus, collected 15 tons of gold every year (1 Kings 9:27–28)

6. This famous "garden" of Adam and Eve was near a land filled with gold (Genesis 2:10–11)
7. This gift is mentioned in Song of Solomon as a perfume (Song of Solomon 3:6)
8. A shortened form of the third gift

Down

1. This man, who once visited Jesus at night, brought myrrh for Jesus' body (John 19:39)
3. This is the first gift mentioned in the story of the Wise Men (Matthew 2:11)
5. What the man in 1 Down was preparing Jesus' body for (John 19:40)

21

TAXES AND TAX COLLECTORS

Joseph and Mary had probably told the Wise Men that over a year earlier, Caesar Augustus had given orders that the entire Roman Empire was to pay taxes. Everyone in Israel had to go to their hometown to register and to pay. Because Joseph was originally from Bethlehem, they had left Nazareth and traveled south. It was not a tremendously long journey like the one the Magi had made, but Mary was nearly ready to give birth, so the journey was very difficult for her, and they couldn't travel fast.

The Wise Men understood all about paying taxes to the Romans. Remember, they'd had to pay taxes when they first entered the Roman Empire. The Bible tells several stories about taxes and tax collectors. (Jesus said more about them than anyone else!) Try to answer the following questions about taxes in Bible times.

1. King Saul said that whoever _____, his family wouldn't have to pay taxes.
   a) loaned him some money
   b) married his daughter
   c) gave to charity
   d) killed Goliath

2. Pharaoh demanded silver and gold, and King Jehoiakim got it by taxing _____.
   a) the people of Egypt
   b) the people of Judah
   c) the priests
   d) tax collectors

3. In Nehemiah's day, many Jews _____ to pay taxes on their fields and vineyards.
   a) wrote a check
   b) used their savings
   c) borrowed money
   d) canceled their vacations

4. Amos said Israel's greedy rulers even made poor people pay a tax on _____.
   a) their straw
   b) their hair
   c) their sandals
   d) their gold

5. John the Baptist told the tax collectors not to collect any more
_____.
   a) taxes
   b) stamps
   c) than they had to
   d) garbage

6. People despised tax collectors, but Jesus said that even tax collectors
_____.
   a) washed their dirty dishes
   b) bathed twice a week
   c) fed their dogs every day
   d) loved those who loved them

7. Which one of Jesus' twelve disciples used to be a tax collector?
   a) Matthew
   b) Peter
   c) Bartholomew
   d) Judas

8. Where did Jesus tell Peter he would find a coin to pay the temple tax?
   a) inside his shoe
   b) on the temple steps
   c) in a fish's mouth
   d) under his bed

9. When a tax collector went up to the temple to pray, what did he say to God?
  a) "I thank You that I am not like other men."
  b) "I did better this week, God."
  c) "God, have mercy on me, a sinner."
  d) "Help me earn more money."

10. Which tax collector climbed a tree to see Jesus passing underneath?
  a) Matthew
  b) Zacharias
  c) Zacchaeus
  d) Tarzan

11. Jesus told the _____ that tax collectors entered the kingdom of God before them.
  a) chief priests
  b) gluttons
  c) drunkards
  d) prostitutes

12. Jesus' tricky enemies asked Him if it was right to pay taxes to _____ or not.
  a) the temple
  b) Caesar
  c) Caiaphas
  d) the IRS

ANSWERS

1. d) killed Goliath (1 Samuel 17:23–25 NIV)
2. b) the people of Judah (2 Kings 23:34–35 NLT)
3. c) borrowed money (Nehemiah 5:4)
4. a) their straw (Amos 5:11 NKJV)
5. c) than they had to (Luke 3:2, 11–13)
6. d) loved those who loved them (Matthew 5:46)
7. a) Matthew (Matthew 9:9)
8. c) in a fish's mouth (Matthew 17:24–27)
9. c) "God, have mercy on me, a sinner." (Luke 18:10, 13 NIV)
10. c) Zacchaeus (Luke 19:1–4)
11. a) chief priests (Matthew 21:23, 31)
12. b) Caesar (Matthew 22:15–17)

Did you get the last answer right? And what did Jesus answer? He said that yes, it *was* right to pay taxes to Caesar (the Roman government). He said to "give to Caesar what belongs to Caesar, and give to God what belongs to God" (Matthew 22:21 NLT). You should be honest and pay the authorities whatever you owe. The apostle Paul added, "Give to everyone what you owe them: If you owe taxes, pay taxes" (Romans 13:7 NIV).

Now, you're probably too young to pay taxes, but the principle still applies. If you owe somebody some money, be sure that you pay them back. Don't just hope that they forget about it. Or if you borrowed a book or video game from a friend, make sure to return it.

And, very importantly, when you go to church, remember to "give to God what belongs to God."

22

FARM ANIMALS

By the time the Wise Men arrived in Bethlehem, it was several months—probably over a year—since Jesus had been born. Mary and Joseph had long ago moved out of the stable. Just the same, the Magi were probably shocked to learn that when Jesus' parents had come to Bethlehem, it was so crowded with people who'd come to pay taxes, that there was no room left in the inn. As a result, the King of the Jews had been born in a stable.

Mary wrapped her newborn baby in warm cloths, but there was no bed to lay Him in. There was only a manger filled with straw. A manger is a feed trough for cattle. We don't know how many different farm animals were in the stable that night, but let's have a look at some of the animals that Israelites owned.

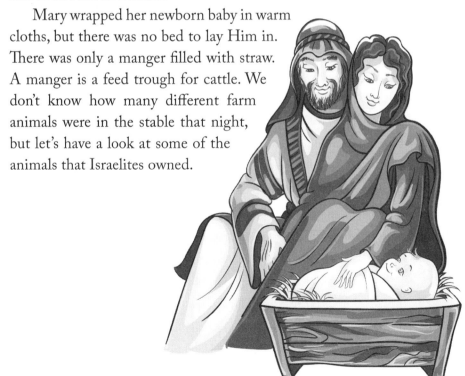

1. Jacob built a house for himself in Sukkoth and made _____ for his livestock.
   a) a corral
   b) shelters
   c) horse blankets
   d) little booties

2. Job used _____ to help the shepherds guard his flocks.
   a) rams
   b) tame bears
   c) dogs
   d) penguins

3. Israelites considered _____ unclean and didn't raise them.
   a) goats
   b) fish
   c) chickens
   d) pigs

4. Nathan told a story about a man who raised _____ just like one of his children.
   a) one ewe lamb
   b) a small dog
   c) a Siamese cat
   d) a gerbil

5. King David put Obil, an Ishmaelite from Arabia, in charge of
_____.
   a) Arabian horses
   b) camels
   c) hunting falcons
   d) rabbits

6. The governors of Israel supplied _____ for Solomon's royal horses
in the stables.
   a) horseshoes
   b) sugar cubes
   c) green grass
   d) barley and straw

7. Proverbs says, "You shall have enough _____ milk for your food..."
   a) cows'
   b) goats'
   c) camels'
   d) chocolate

8. When the prophet Elijah met Elisha, what farm chore was Elisha
doing?
   a) gathering eggs
   b) milking a goat
   c) plowing with oxen
   d) slopping the hogs

9. Every Sabbath day the Jews led their oxen or donkeys from the stall

_____.

   a) to water them

   b) to exercise them

   c) to sell them

   d) to work in their fields

10. Jesus said, "I am sending you out as sheep among wolves. So be as . . .harmless as _____."

   a) sheep

   b) kittens

   c) doves

   d) serpents

11. Jesus sent His disciples into a village ahead of Him to borrow _____.

   a) a mule

   b) a young donkey

   c) an ostrich

   d) a goose

12. Jesus wanted to gather Jerusalem's children as a _____ gathers her chicks under her wings.

   a) eagle

   b) falcon

   c) nightingale

   d) hen

ANSWERS

1. b) shelters (Genesis 33:17 NIV)
2. c) dogs (Job 30:1)
3. d) pigs (Leviticus 11:7–8)
4. a) one ewe lamb (2 Samuel 12:1–3)
5. b) camels (1 Chronicles 27:30)
6. d) barley and straw (1 Kings 4:27–28 NLT)
7. b) goats' (Proverbs 27:27 NKJV)
8. c) plowing with oxen (1 Kings 19:19)
9. a) to water them (Luke 13:15)
10. c) doves (Matthew 10:16 nlt)
11. b) a young donkey (Luke 19:28–35 nlt)
12. d) hen (Matthew 23:37)

As you probably learned from these last questions, Jewish farmers did things a little differently thousands of years ago than farmers do today. For example, they had teams of oxen to pull their plows instead of tractors. And where did they *keep* these valuable animals at night, so that nobody stole them? Larger homes had a small courtyard where the oxen slept—usually under a covered porch on the east wall.

Farmers also kept their animals in caves, to keep them out of the rain and cold. To this day, there are many caves in the limestone cliffs around Bethlehem, and the stable that Jesus was born in was probably just such a cave. The cattle may indeed have been lowing (as the carol "Away in a Manger" says), but it is doubtful that the ox was actually keeping time to a boy playing on his drum.

23

SEEING ANGELS

The Wise Men also learned that they weren't the first people to come to honor the newborn King. A group of shepherds living in fields near Bethlehem had been the first. As a Christmas carol says: "While shepherds watched their flocks by night, all seated on the ground, the angel of the Lord came down, and glory shone around."

The angel told them, "Do not be afraid, for behold, I bring you good tidings of great joy which will be to all people. For there is born to you this day in the city of David a Savior, who is Christ the Lord" (Luke 2:10–11 NKJV). Suddenly the sky filled with angels praising God. After the angels left, the shepherds hurried to Bethlehem and found the baby.

The shepherds were the first to come see Jesus. However, they weren't the first people to see *angels*.

1. Who was the first person in the Bible to see the angel of the Lord?
   a) Angela
   b) Abraham
   c) Moses
   d) Hagar

2. What did the two angels do to the men who attacked Lot's house?
   a) knocked them down
   b) struck them blind
   c) chased them away
   d) tied them up in a fishnet

3. Jacob had a dream about a tall ladder. What were angels doing on the ladder?
   a) putting stars in the sky
   b) painting a rainbow
   c) going up and down
   d) carrying packages

4. Joshua met a powerful angel. What was the first thing the angel told him to do?
   a) take off his sandals
   b) march around Jericho
   c) be silent
   d) shout and blow trumpets

5. When Gideon first saw the angel of the Lord, what was the angel doing?
   a) threshing wheat
   b) holding a sword
   c) sitting under a tree
   d) riding a chariot

6. What did the angel of the Lord do while Manoah and his wife watched?
   a) told Manoah to build an ark
   b) began glowing brightly
   c) caused a hailstorm
   d) rose to heaven in a flame

7. Daniel saw an angel by the Tigris River. What did the angel's face look like?
   a) a lion
   b) lightning
   c) a mighty rushing wind
   d) a movie star

8. What was the name of the angel who appeared to both Zacharias and Mary?
   a) Michael
   b) Gabriel
   c) Sanhedrin
   d) Cherub

9. What was Mary Magdalene doing when she saw two angels in Jesus' tomb?
   a) weeping
   b) entering the tomb
   c) praying
   d) talking with Peter

10. When Peter was in prison, an angel appeared to him. What did the angel do?
   a) caused an earthquake
   b) began singing hymns
   c) opened the prison doors
   d) gave him a vision

11. Where was Paul when an angel appeared to him during a terrible storm?
   a) by the rivers of Babylon
   b) standing on the seashore
   c) on a ship at sea
   d) climbing a ladder

12. John saw seven angels standing before God. What was given to each of them?
   a) a golden harp
   b) a trumpet
   c) a halo
   d) a little book

ANSWERS

1. d) Hagar (Genesis 16:7–13)
2. b) struck them blind (Genesis 19:1–11)
3. c) going up and down (Genesis 28:10–12 NKJV)
4. a) take off his sandals (Joshua 5:13–15)
5. c) sitting under a tree (Judges 6:11–12)
6. d) rose to heaven in a flame (Judges 13:19–20)
7. b) lightning (Daniel 10:4–6)
8. b) Gabriel (Luke 1:18–19, 26–27)
9. a) weeping (John 20:11–12)
10. c) opened the prison doors (Acts 12:5–10)
11. c) on a ship at sea (Acts 27:18–24)
12. b) a trumpet (Revelation 8:2)

If you've never heard some of these stories before, take the time to look them up and read them now. Angels are fascinating otherworldly beings, and everyone in the Bible who saw an angel was changed forever. Sometimes, when angels appeared to men and women, the angels shone with heavenly glory. The shepherds outside Bethlehem immediately knew that they were seeing angels of God.

Other times, angels walked among human beings, seeming to be just men. For example, Lot met two strangers in the city square and kindly invited them into his house. He thought they were ordinary travelers. Only later did he find out they were powerful, immortal beings! That's another good reason to be kind to strangers: they might be angels in disguise (see Hebrews 13:2).

24

PROPHECIES ABOUT JESUS

The angel told the shepherds that "a Savior, who is Christ the Lord" had been born "in the city of David" (Luke 2:11 NKJV). That city was Bethlehem. Hundreds of years earlier, Micah had prophesied that the Ruler of Israel would come from Bethlehem (Micah 5:2). As we have seen, Jesus fulfilled Micah's prophecy when He was born in that very place.

Also, Gabriel had told Mary that God would give Jesus the throne of His ancestor David, and that He would reign over Israel forever (Luke 1:32–33). That was another prophecy that the Savior had to fulfill—He had to be a descendant of King David of old. And Jesus was. That's why people often called Him "Son of David."

Jesus also fulfilled many *more* ancient prophecies that the Savior had to fulfill. It's time to find out how well you know them.

1. Jesus taught and did miracles in Galilee (Matthew 4:12–16; Luke 4:31–34). This fulfilled a prophecy that the people of Galilee who sat in darkness would _____.
   a) make great changes
   b) receive God's Spirit
   c) see a great light
   d) stand up

2. Jesus fulfilled this prophecy: "The LORD has said to Me, 'You are My _____'" (Psalm 2:7 NKJV).
   a) Son
   b) road sign
   c) dove
   d) salt of the earth

3. David prophesied: "I will open my mouth in a parable" (Psalm 78:2 NKJV). Who told more parables than anyone else?
   a) David
   b) Solomon
   c) Zechariah
   d) Jesus

4. When Jesus rode a donkey into Jerusalem (Matthew 21:1–5), which prophecy did He fulfill?
   a) "The LORD will guide you continually." (Isaiah 58:11 NKJV)
   b) "Let us go into the house of the LORD." (Psalm 122:1 NKJV)
   c) "Your King is coming to you. . .on a donkey." (Zechariah 9:9 NKJV)
   d) "Issachar is a strong donkey." (Genesis 49:14 NKJV)

5. The prophecy "Strike the Shepherd, and the sheep will be scattered" (Zechariah 13:7 NKJV) was fulfilled when Jesus' disciples _____.
   a) went out preaching
   b) forsook Him in the Garden
   c) were watching sheep
   d) were scatterbrained

6. David wrote: "...for My clothing they cast lots" (Psalm 22:18 NKJV). How was this fulfilled?
   a) David donated his clothes to charity.
   b) Joseph's brothers ripped his colorful robe.
   c) Samson stole the Philistine's clothing.
   d) The soldiers gambled for Jesus' clothing.

7. Isaiah wrote: "He was numbered with the transgressors" (Isaiah 53:12 NKJV). How did Jesus fulfill this?
   a) He chose Judas as a disciple.
   b) He was a friend of sinners.
   c) He was crucified with thieves.
   d) He took our sins on the cross.

8. Isaiah prophesied, "Who has believed our report?" (Isaiah 53:1 NKJV) Even though Jesus had done many miracles, some Jews didn't _____.
   a) believe in Him
   b) see the miracles
   c) believe in miracles
   d) do miracles

9. Which king prophesied about Jesus' crucifixion, "They pierced My hands and My feet"?
   a) Saul
   b) David
   c) Ahab
   d) Caiaphas

10. The Romans broke the leg bones of the crucified thieves. They didn't break Jesus' legs (John 19:31–36). Which verse did this fulfill?
   a) "My bones are pierced in me at night." (Job 30:17 NKJV)
   b) ". . .the bones You have broken may rejoice." (Psalm 51:8 NKJV)
   c) "He guards all his bones; not one of them is broken." (Psalm 34:20 NKJV)
   d) "Son of man, can these bones live?" (Ezekiel 37:3 NKJV)

11. Isaiah prophesied, "They made His grave. . .with the rich at His death" (Isaiah 53:9 NKJV). _____ was the rich man in whose tomb Jesus was buried.
   a) Solomon
   b) Joseph of Arimathea
   c) Nicodemus
   d) The rich young ruler

12. David prophesied, "You will not leave my soul in Sheol [the grave]" (Psalm 16:10 NKJV). When did Jesus fulfill this?
   a) when He was born
   b) when He was baptized
   c) when He was raised from the dead
   d) when He was buried in a grave

ANSWERS

1. c) see a great light (Isaiah 9:1–2)
2. a) Son (Mark 1:11)
3. d) Jesus (Matthew 13:31–35)
4. c) "Your King is coming to you. . .on a donkey." (Zechariah 9:9 NKJV)
5. b) forsook Him in the Garden (Matthew 26:31, 56)
6. d) The soldiers gambled for Jesus' clothing. (Matthew 27:35)
7. c) He was crucified with thieves. (Mark 15:27–28)
8. a) believe in Him (John 12:37–38)
9. b) David (Psalm 22:16 NKJV)
10. c) "He guards all his bones; not one of them is broken." (Psalm 34:20 NKJV)
11. b) Joseph of Arimathea (Matthew 27:57–60)
12. c) when He was raised from the dead (Acts 2:22–32)

If you know the story of Jesus well, you probably got many of these answers right. But did you know that by doing these things Jesus fulfilled the words of many ancient prophets? Yes, Jesus' birth, life, death, and resurrection fulfilled more than 360 Old Testament prophecies. The Wise Men had just met Him and were learning about the amazing prophecies this young child had *already* fulfilled.

God predicted exactly what His Son would do so that the Jewish people would recognize who He was and accept Him as the Savior. God also had His prophets write things down for *our* sake. The Bible says that Jesus' words and deeds "are written that you may believe that Jesus is the Christ, the Son of God, and that believing you may have life in His name" (John 20:31 NKJV).

25

THE JEWISH TEMPLE

Forty days after Jesus was born, Joseph and Mary took Him to the temple in Jerusalem. They went there for two reasons. The first was to present a sacrifice for Mary, because she had just had a child. Usually families sacrificed a lamb. The second reason they were there was to present Jesus, their firstborn son, to God. Again, families normally sacrificed a lamb (Exodus 13:12–13).

The problem was that Joseph and Mary had almost no money. Joseph was no longer working at his carpentry shop in Nazareth and couldn't afford a lamb—let alone two lambs. Fortunately, the Law of Moses allowed poor people to sacrifice a pair of doves or two pigeons instead (Leviticus 12:6–8). So that's what Joseph and Mary offered.

The Jewish people were often at the temple. They went there to offer sacrifices to God, to attend religious festivals, and simply to pray. How much do you know about this place of worship?

1. Who wanted to build a temple for God but wasn't allowed to?
   a) Saul
   b) David
   c) Balaam
   d) a Templar Knight

2. How many years did it take King Solomon to build the temple?
   a) seven years
   b) fourteen years
   c) twenty-one years
   d) forty years

3. The inside walls of the temple were cedar boards. What was carved on them?
   a) nothing at all
   b) cherubim and angels
   c) cherubim, palm trees, and flowers
   d) the names of the builders

4. What was kept in the most holy place, the innermost room of the temple?
   a) twenty golden shields
   b) the altar of incense
   c) the high priest's robes
   d) the ark of the covenant

5. What was the name of the boy who hid in the temple for six years?
   a) John the Baptist
   b) Moses
   c) Joash
   d) Gideon

6. Evil kings put things for false gods in the temple. What good king took them out?
   a) Good King Wenceslas
   b) King Henry VII
   c) King of the South
   d) King Josiah

7. Who was in charge of rebuilding the temple after it was destroyed?
   a) Zacharias and Elizabeth
   b) Zerubbabel and Jeshua
   c) James and Andrew
   d) Samson

8. What twelve-year-old boy spent three days in the temple talking to the teachers?
   a) Pinocchio
   b) Larry the Cucumber
   c) Jesus
   d) Paul's nephew

9. What was Zacharias doing in the temple when he saw the angel Gabriel?

  a) praying
  b) sacrificing a lamb
  c) arguing with Caiaphas
  d) burning incense

10. Jesus made a whip and used it to drive _____ out of the temple.

  a) money changers and merchants
  b) tax collectors and farmers
  c) the temple guards
  d) the scribes and Pharisees

11. Jesus said that one day every stone of the temple would be _____.

  a) perfectly square
  b) used as the cornerstone
  c) thrown down
  d) covered with gold

12. What did Paul's enemies falsely accuse him of bringing into the temple?

  a) dogs
  b) pigs
  c) Greeks
  d) a sack of potatoes

ANSWERS

1. b) David (2 Samuel 7:1–13)
2. a) seven years (1 Kings 6:37–38)
3. c) cherubim, palm trees, and flowers (1 Kings 6:14–15, 29)
4. d) the ark of the covenant (1 Kings 8:6)
5. c) Joash (2 Kings 11:1–3)
6. d) King Josiah (2 Kings 22:1–7; 23:4)
7. b) Zerubbabel and Jeshua (Ezra 3:8; 5:2)
8. c) Jesus (Luke 2:41–46)
9. d) burning incense (Luke 1:8–11)
10. a) money changers and merchants (John 2:13–16)
11. c) thrown down (Matthew 24:1–2)
12. c) Greeks (Acts 21:27–29)

In Jesus' day, God's temple at Jerusalem was one of the most magnificent buildings on earth. Herod was an ungodly king, but he loved to build, so he took apart the temple and built a much greater one in its place. A Jewish book, the Talmud, said that he who had not seen the temple of Herod had never in his life seen a beautiful building.

Herod's temple was even more awe-inspiring than the one Solomon had built. Its massive stone walls rose above Jerusalem, and its gold-covered rooftops were dazzling in the sunlight. And once you climbed up the steps and stood in the wide temple courts, you were overwhelmed by the buildings towering above you. Even Jesus' disciples were impressed by the temple. But instead of looking around in awe, Jesus told them that all these fine buildings would be torn down (Matthew 24:1–2).

26

PROPHETS AND PROPHETESSES

The shepherds were the first people to see Jesus and realize that He was the Savior, the King of the Jews. But were the Wise Men the *next* ones to see Jesus and to realize who He was? No, they weren't. As you just learned, forty days after Jesus was born, Joseph and Mary took Him to the temple. While they were there, an old man named Simeon saw them. He walked up, took Jesus in his arms, and prophesied that He was the Savior and the light of all nations (Luke 2:25–32). At that instant, an old prophetess named Anna also came in, saw Jesus, and told everyone that He was the Savior (Luke 2:36–38).

There were many other true prophets and prophetesses in the Bible, besides Simeon and Anna. Let's see how well you know them.

1. God told the Philistine king Abimelech to return this prophet's wife to him.
   a) Adam
   b) Elijah
   c) Daniel
   d) Abraham

2. This singer, the sister of Aaron, was the first prophetess mentioned in the Bible.
   a) Jehosheba
   b) Hoglah
   c) Miriam
   d) Mara

3. Moses' face glowed with light after he _____ for forty days.
   a) stood in the sunshine
   b) washed his face
   c) talked with God
   d) was hit by lightning

4. The prophetess Deborah used to sit _____ when she judged Israel.
   a) on a fancy chair
   b) under a palm tree
   c) in a chariot
   d) nowhere

5. When God first spoke to him, the boy Samuel thought it was
_____ talking.
   a) old Eli
   b) his mother
   c) an angel
   d) God

6. The prophet Elijah hid in the canyon of a small creek. Who brought
him food?
   a) pizza delivery
   b) the widow of Zarephath
   c) birds
   d) raccoons

7. This prophet put flour into a pot of poisoned stew, and it became
safe to eat.
   a) Pharaoh's baker
   b) the apostle Paul
   c) Captain Cook
   d) Elisha

8. A terrified captain asked this prophet, "How can you sleep at a time
like this?"
   a) John the Baptist
   b) Jonah
   c) Jonathan
   d) Joshua

9. The prophetess Huldah said God would have mercy on Josiah because he was _____.
   a) the king
   b) her cousin
   c) an Israelite
   d) tenderhearted

10. What did a kind African man rescue the prophet Jeremiah from?
    a) a hungry lion
    b) a muddy pit
    c) the Nile River
    d) a charging elephant

11. In a vision, an angel grabbed the prophet Ezekiel by _____ and lifted him up.
    a) his hair
    b) his big toe
    c) his hand
    d) his belt

12. The prophet Agabus warned that a great worldwide _____ was coming.
    a) earthquake
    b) flood
    c) famine
    d) hailstorm

ANSWERS

1. d) Abraham (Genesis 20:1–7)
2. c) Miriam (Exodus 15:20–21)
3. c) talked with God (Exodus 34:29)
4. b) under a palm tree (Judges 4:4–5 NKJV)
5. a) old Eli (1 Samuel 3:2–5)
6. c) birds (1 Kings 17:2–6)
7. d) Elisha (2 Kings 4:38–41 NKJV)
8. b) Jonah (Jonah 1:4–6 NLT)
9. d) tenderhearted (2 Kings 22:1, 11–20)
10. b) a muddy pit (Jeremiah 38:4–13)
11. a) his hair (Ezekiel 8:1–3)
12. c) famine (Acts 11:27–28 NKJV)

Were you surprised to learn that there were several prophetesses in the Bible? Normally, when we think of Bible prophets, we think of bushy-bearded men like Moses and Elijah, with wild hair and rough clothing. But the Lord is not limited to using men. His Holy Spirit inspired both men *and* women to prophesy the words of God in Old Testament times.

And He spoke through women even *more* in New Testament times. He had promised, "And it shall come to pass in the last days, says God, that I will pour out of My Spirit on all flesh; your sons and your daughters shall prophesy" (Acts 2:17 NKJV). Here's a bonus question for you: Philip the evangelist had four daughters. How many of them prophesied? (a) one, (b) two, (c) three, (d) four. The answer, as you probably guessed, is (d) four (see Acts 21:8–9).

27

JOBS IN BIBLE TIMES

Joseph and Mary had traveled south to pay their taxes, but they didn't return north to Nazareth right away. They were still living in Bethlehem about a year or so later when the Wise Men came. It was a good thing they stayed. If they hadn't, when the Magi finally arrived in Israel, they'd never have found the baby Jesus.

Joseph and Mary probably had very practical reasons for not leaving. Mary couldn't make a long trip for several weeks after giving birth—and during that time they needed money to live on. They'd used up all of their savings when paying their taxes. So Joseph had probably started doing carpentry work in Bethlehem and ended up so busy that they decided to move into a house and stay there.

Bible people worked at many different kinds of jobs back then, as you shall see.

1. Four of Jesus' twelve disciples used to _____ as a full-time job.
   a) work on farms
   b) collect taxes
   c) catch fish
   d) work as carpenters

2. Jesus told a parable in which He was a farmer who planted _____.
   a) beets
   b) corn
   c) good seed
   d) turnips

3. Faithful Jews didn't eat pork, so only the most desperate Jew worked as a _____.
   a) banker
   b) butcher
   c) chef
   d) swineherd

4. Hosea said that a _____ kept his oven hot after kneading the dough.
   a) pizza cook
   b) baker
   c) five-star chef
   d) armorer

5. Jeremiah went to a _____ shop and watched him working at his wheel.

   a) wheel maker's

   b) chariot maker's

   c) mechanic's

   d) potter's

6. King Hezekiah said, "My life. . .has been cut short, as when a weaver cuts _____."

   a) cloth from a loom

   b) a rug in half

   c) up carrots

   d) a sandal strap

7. When he appears, _____ will be like a laundry washer's soap.

   a) the Prodigal Son

   b) the Lord

   c) the older brother

   d) Mr. Clean

8. Isaiah said that this workman "fans the coals into flame and forges a weapon."

   a) forger

   b) coal miner

   c) blacksmith

   d) fireman

9. This man, who normally created beautiful things, helped build Jerusalem's walls.

    a) songwriter

    b) painter

    c) toy maker

    d) goldsmith

10. Solomon had many _____ cut stones for God's temple.

    a) stonemasons

    b) carpenters

    c) stone saws

    d) college graduates

11. Luke, who wrote the Gospel of Luke, worked for years as a _____.

    a) fisherman

    b) doctor

    c) centurion

    d) pro wrestler

12. The Bible says some enemy soldiers _____ like woodcutters in a forest.

    a) swung their axes

    b) fought bravely

    c) sang out of tune

    d) killed big bad wolves

ANSWERS

1. c) catch fish (Mark 1:16–20)
2. c) good seed (Matthew 13:37)
3. d) swineherd (Leviticus 11:7–8; Luke 15:11–15)
4. b) baker (Hosea 7:4)
5. d) potter's (Jeremiah 18:1–3)
6. a) cloth from a loom (Isaiah 38:12 NLT)
7. b) the Lord (Malachi 3:1–2)
8. c) blacksmith (Isaiah 54:16 NIV)
9. d) goldsmith (Nehemiah 2:17–18; 3:31)
10. a) stonemasons (1 Chronicles 22:2, 15)
11. b) doctor (Colossians 4:14)
12. a) swung their axes (Psalm 74:4–5 NLT)

The Wise Men came seeking the King of the Jews. The child they found was that and much more: Jesus was the King over all kings and Lord over all lords (Revelation 19:16). Yet Jesus was born in a cow's shed, not a palace. And instead of being pampered as a royal prince, He worked hard as a carpenter (Mark 6:1–3). Instead of being waited upon by servants, Jesus came to serve others. "For even the Son of Man did not come to be served, but to serve, and to give his life as a ransom for many" (Mark 10:45 NIV).

You have to wonder what the Wise Men thought as they sat in Joseph and Mary's humble house and saw Jesus dressed like an ordinary carpenter's son. Little did they know, but the King of the Jews would work for many years as a carpenter Himself.

28

AMAZING DREAMS

God had spoken to Joseph and Mary and others, but so far, God hadn't spoken to the Wise Men. He had led them by a star. But now God *spoke* to them. "And being warned of God in a dream that they should not return to Herod, they departed into their own country another way" (Matthew 2:12). They must have been thrilled to receive divine direction.

The Wise Men had probably traveled to Judea by the northern route. When they returned home, to avoid passing north through Jerusalem, they likely crossed the desert in the south where water was scarce and caravans sometimes got lost. Yet they were so sure that God had spoken to them that they were willing to take this dangerous route.

So the Wise Men joined a long list of Bible people who had heard from God in dreams.

1. In a dream, God told _____, "Indeed you are a dead man."
   a) Abimelech
   b) Pharaoh
   c) Lazarus
   d) Frankenstein

2. Who dreamed about rams (male goats) that were streaked, speckled, and gray spotted?
   a) Daniel
   b) Ramses
   c) Jacob
   d) Aram

3. In a dream, God told _____, "Be careful that you speak to Jacob neither good nor bad."
   a) Rachel
   b) Esau
   c) Leah
   d) Laban

4. Joseph dreamed that after he tied a bundle of wheat together, it _____.
   a) started speaking
   b) turned silver
   c) rose and stood up
   d) fell apart again

5. Where were Pharaoh's butler and baker when they had their amazing dreams?
   a) in their beds
   b) in prison
   c) in the garden
   d) driving chariots

6. In a dream, _____ came out of the Nile River and ate seven fat cows.
   a) crocodiles
   b) hippopotamuses
   c) warthogs
   d) skinny cows

7. Who was happy to hear a dream about a loaf of bread knocking down a tent?
   a) Gideon
   b) Pharaoh's baker
   c) Joshua
   d) the Wise Men

8. God appeared to _____ in a dream and said, "Ask! What shall I give you?"
   a) Adam
   b) Solomon
   c) the merchant seeking pearls
   d) Queen Esther

9. Who had a dream and insisted that his wise men tell him what he had dreamed?

   a) Noah

   b) Nebuchadnezzar

   c) Herod

   d) Walt Disney

10. Daniel once dreamed about a leopard. What did it have on its back?

   a) lots of spots

   b) a woman dressed in scarlet

   c) four wings

   d) a superhero cape

11. In a dream, God told Joseph (Mary's husband) that it was now safe to go here.

   a) Herod's palace

   b) the supermarket

   c) Egypt

   d) Israel

12. Who suffered many things in a dream because of Jesus?

   a) Pilate

   b) Pilate's wife

   c) Herod Antipas

   d) Governor Felix

ANSWERS

1. a) Abimelech (Genesis 20:3 NKJV)
2. c) Jacob (Genesis 31:10–12 NKJV)
3. d) Laban (Genesis 31:24 NKJV)
4. c) rose and stood up (Genesis 37:5–7)
5. b) in prison (Genesis 40:5)
6. d) skinny cows (Genesis 41:17–21)
7. a) Gideon (Judges 7:9–15)
8. b) Solomon (1 Kings 3:5 NKJV)
9. b) Nebuchadnezzar (Daniel 2:1–6)
10. c) four wings (Daniel 7:1, 6)
11. d) Israel (Matthew 2:19–21)
12. b) Pilate's wife (Matthew 27:17–19)

How many of these questions did you know the answers to? How many did you have to simply guess the answers to? Sometimes dreams are like that. They're full of strange scenes and jumbled-up events, and we have no idea what they mean. Sometimes we wonder if they mean anything at all.

Most of the time, our dreams are *not* messages from God. We're only dreaming about things we were thinking about during the day. As the Bible says, "A dream comes when there are many cares" (Ecclesiastes 5:3 NIV).

But God *does* sometimes speak to us in dreams—and if He does, we usually know it, because it will be so clear. "He speaks in dreams, in visions of the night, when deep sleep falls on people as they lie in their beds" (Job 33:15 NLT). However, we may still have to pray about what it *means*.

29

EGYPT IN THE BIBLE

Shortly after the Wise Men left—probably the following night—an angel warned Joseph in a dream that Herod would try to kill Jesus, and urged him to flee with his family to Egypt (Matthew 2:13). So he and Mary hastily packed and left their house in Bethlehem that same night, while their neighbors were sleeping.

Why did the angel tell them to go to Egypt? Because it was just far enough away to be out of Herod's reach. Plus, there were many Jews living all over Egypt, in the cities and in the countryside and along the Nile River. There were over one million Jews in the city of Alexandria alone. One more small Jewish family would never be noticed.

Throughout their history, the Jews had a lot to do with the land of the pharaohs, and the Bible talks a lot about Egypt.

1. Abraham went down to Egypt because the land of Canaan had
_____.
   a) giants
   b) high taxes
   c) a famine
   d) too many people

2. God sent plagues on Pharaoh because he had taken Abraham's
_____.
   a) camels
   b) gold and silver
   c) nephew
   d) wife

3. Pharaoh gave _____ great power and a new name: Zaphnathpaaneah.
   a) Joseph
   b) Zaphnath
   c) Ishbibenob
   d) Zerubbabel

4. After meeting this wrinkled old man, Pharaoh asked him, "How old are you?"
   a) Methuselah
   b) Jacob
   c) Abraham
   d) Gandalf

5. Pharaoh made the Hebrew slaves build _____ out of stone.
   a) the Pyramids
   b) the Sphinx
   c) the Great Wall of China
   d) two cities

6. Moses' mother put him in a bulrush ark. Then where did she set the ark?
   a) drifting on the Nile River
   b) among reeds by the riverbank
   c) in the Dead Sea
   d) safely in her bedroom

7. What did the children of Israel like the most about Egypt?
   a) sunset on the Nile
   b) cucumbers and melons
   c) the hard work
   d) swimming with crocodiles

8. Which king of Israel married a princess of Egypt?
   a) David
   b) the prince of Egypt
   c) Balthazar
   d) Solomon

9. When Rehoboam was king of Judah, Pharaoh Shishak of Egypt attacked _____.
   a) Jerusalem
   b) Bethlehem
   c) Babylon
   d) New York

10. Pharaoh Necho changed Prince Eliakim's name and made him the new _____.
   a) court jester
   b) Pharaoh
   c) king of Judah
   d) pop star

11. Which prophet didn't want to go to Egypt but was taken there anyway?
   a) Jeremiah
   b) Moses
   c) Jonah
   d) Simon Peter

12. What did God compare Pharaoh, king of Egypt, to?
   a) a fat pumpkin
   b) a lazy stork
   c) a great river monster
   d) a fly on the wall

ANSWERS

1. c) a famine (Genesis 12:4–5, 10)
2. d) wife (Genesis 12:11–20)
3. a) Joseph (Genesis 41:45)
4. b) Jacob (Genesis 47:7–8 NKJV)
5. d) two cities (Exodus 1:11)
6. b) among reeds by the riverbank (Exodus 2:1–3 NKJV)
7. b) cucumbers and melons (Numbers 11:4–5)
8. d) Solomon (1 Kings 3:1)
9. a) Jerusalem (1 Kings 14:25)
10. c) king of Judah (2 Kings 23:31–34)
11. a) Jeremiah (Jeremiah 43:1–7)
12. c) a great river monster (Ezekiel 29:1–5 NKJV)

It was fortunate that the Wise Men had given Jesus such generous gifts. Joseph and Mary were able to use the gold to buy food and to rent a house in Egypt. The Bible doesn't tell us how long they had to stay there. After a couple of months, however, they may have also sold the frankincense and myrrh for money to live on, until Joseph could find steady work.

After King Herod died, an angel told Joseph in a dream that it was safe to return and that he should arise and take the young child and his mother back home to Israel. So, like Moses and the children of Israel, Mary and Joseph and Jesus left Egypt to go to the Promised Land. Matthew's Gospel says that this fulfilled a prophecy given centuries earlier: "Out of Egypt I called My Son" (Hosea 11:1; Matthew 2:15 NKJV).

30

CHANGED LIVES

The Wise Men had gone to Israel to show respect and honor to an important earthly ruler—the King of the Jews—but had found the Son of God Himself. When they "departed for their own country" (Matthew 2:12 NKJV), they had plenty to talk about on the long trip home. And when they finally arrived back in Parthia, perhaps all their friends and townspeople who had seen them leave on their quest many months earlier flocked around them to hear their stories. And such stories they had to tell!

Their lives had been forever changed by their great adventure. The Bible describes several other people whose lives were changed through an encounter with Jesus. Let's see how familiar you are with the following men and women.

1. Jesus called Matthew to follow Him. Then He said He'd come to call _____ to repent.
   a) tax collectors
   b) publicans
   c) sinners
   d) the righteous

2. Simon Peter confessed that he was a sinful man then immediately _____.
   a) said he wasn't
   b) sinned again
   c) went fishing
   d) followed Jesus

3. Jesus cast seven devils out of _____.
She then became Jesus' close disciple.
   a) Joanna
   b) Mary Magdalene
   c) Susanna
   d) Pilate's wife

4. Jesus told a man to tell his friends what the Lord had done for him. The man told _____.
   a) no one
   b) just his friends
   c) his friends and family
   d) the whole city

5. After Jesus healed him, this man said, "Lord, I believe!" and worshiped Jesus.
   a) a man born blind
   b) a leper
   c) a paralyzed man
   d) a deaf-mute man

6. When this short rich man repented, Jesus said, "Today salvation has come to this house."
   a) Pepin the Short
   b) Thaddeus
   c) Zacchaeus
   d) Bilbo Baggins

7. This blind man wouldn't stop shouting to Jesus and later happily followed Him.
   a) Bartholomew
   b) Bartimaeus
   c) Timaeus
   d) Timothy

8. He persecuted Christians until he saw Jesus. He later preferred to be called Paul.
   a) Herodias
   b) Festus
   c) Saul
   d) Tarsus

9. This important Roman centurion was one of the first non-Jewish Christians.

    a) Cornelius

    b) Maximilian

    c) Maximus

    d) Romanus

10. This governor of Cyprus believed in Jesus after a sorcerer was miraculously blinded.

    a) Pontius Pilate

    b) Sergius Paulus

    c) Paul Paulus

    d) Cyrus Cyprus

11. _____ put his faith in Jesus after an earthquake set Paul and Silas free from jail.

    a) The jailor

    b) Silas

    c) The ruler of Philippi

    d) The centurion

12. _____ became a Christian after Paul spoke to the wise Greek philosophers in Athens.

    a) Lydia

    b) Athena

    c) Helen of Troy

    d) Damaris

ANSWERS

1. c) sinners (Matthew 9:9–13)
2. d) followed Jesus (Luke 5:4–11)
3. b) Mary Magdalene (Mark 16:9)
4. d) the whole city (Luke 8:38–39)
5. a) a man born blind (John 9:1–38 NKJV)
6. c) Zacchaeus (Luke 19:8–9 NKJV)
7. b) Bartimaeus (Mark 10:46–52)
8. c) Saul (Acts 9:1–6; 13:9)
9. a) Cornelius (Acts 10:1–48)
10. b) Sergius Paulus (Acts 13:6–12)
11. a) The jailor (Acts 16:22–34)
12. d) Damaris (Acts 17:16–34)

When Paul spoke to the wisest philosophers in Athens, Greece, these sages sat back and listened, but only a few people—such as Dionysius and Damaris—accepted the Gospel and became Christians (Acts 17:32–34). What does this show about the other so-called wise men of Athens? They were well-educated and knowledgeable, but they weren't quite as wise as they *thought* they were.

What a difference between them and the *true* Wise Men. The Magi didn't just sit on their rooftops one night, see the Star of Bethlehem, think *Oh, how interesting!*, and go to bed and forget about it. No. They traveled hundreds of miles, crossing mountains and rivers and deserts, to find Jesus, the King of kings.

As the saying goes, "Wise Men still seek Him." Are you a Wise Man or a Wise Woman?

WISE MEN QUOTE PROPHECY

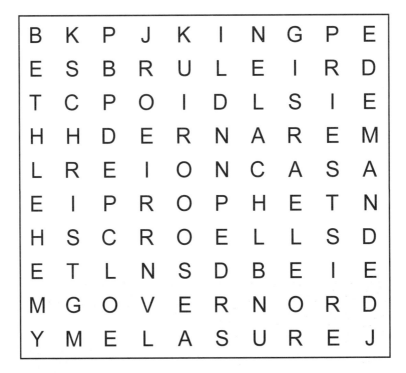

```
B  K  P  J  K  I  N  G  P  E
E  S  B  R  U  L  E  I  R  D
T  C  P  O  I  D  L  S  I  E
H  H  D  E  R  N  A  R  E  M
L  R  E  I  O  N  C  A  S  A
E  I  P  R  O  P  H  E  T  N
H  S  C  R  O  E  L  L  S  D
E  T  L  N  S  D  B  E  I  E
M  G  O  V  E  R  N  O  R  D
Y  M  E  L  A  S  U  R  E  J
```

Find the following **bold-face** words in the puzzle grid above.

When **Herod** the **king** had heard these things, he was troubled, and
all **Jerusalem** with him. And when he had gathered all the chief
priests and scribes of the **people** together, he **demanded** of them
where **Christ** should be **born**. And they said unto him, in **Bethlehem**
of Judaea: for thus it is written by the **prophet**, and thou Bethlehem,
in the land of **Juda**, art not least among the **princes** of Juda: for out of
thee shall come a **Governor**, that shall **rule** my people **Israel**.

MATTHEW 2:3–6

MORE PROPHECIES ABOUT JESUS

The wise men knew a lot about Jesus from Old Testament prophecies. What do you know about those prophecies?

Across
2. Jesus would be this for a dark land (Isaiah 9:2)
5. Jesus would offer this to all people (Isaiah 49:6)
6. This tribe of Israel would produce Jesus (Genesis 49:10)

Down
1. This kind of woman would give birth to Jesus (Isaiah 7:14)
3. Jesus would be the Prince of _____ (Isaiah 9:6)
4. This famous king's throne would belong to Jesus forever (Isaiah 9:7)

ANSWERS FOR CROSSWORD AND WORDSEARCH PUZZLES

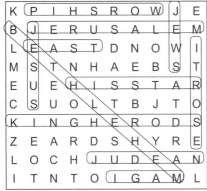

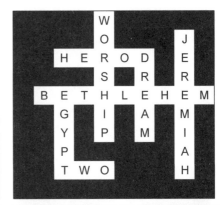

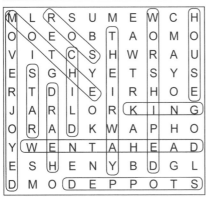

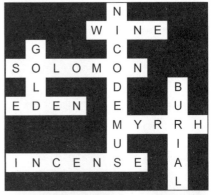

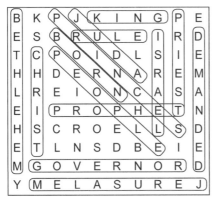

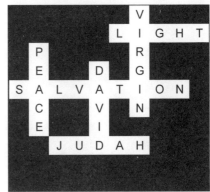

MORE CHRISTMAS ACTIVITY FUN!

WHAT DO YOU KNOW?

A Girl Named Mary

Mary was not just any young woman. God chose her to be the mother of the Christ Child. When God spoke to her, she was willing to do whatever He asked of her. Can you answer these questions?

Whom did God send to Galilee to speak to Mary about the baby she would be having? The answer is hidden in Luke 1:26.

_____

Whom was Mary engaged to when the angel spoke to her? The answer is hidden in Luke 1:27.

_____

Who was the father of Joseph, the husband of Mary, who was Jesus' mother? The answer is hidden in Matthew 1:16.

_____

The angel also told Mary to name her son Jesus, but He would also be called what? The answer is hidden in Luke 1:35.

_____

HOLIDAY SONGS

Find the missing words from the list below.

WINTER _____

GOOD _____ WENCELAS

AWAY IN A _____

HAPPY _____ TO YOU

WHILE _____ WATCHED THEIR FLOCKS

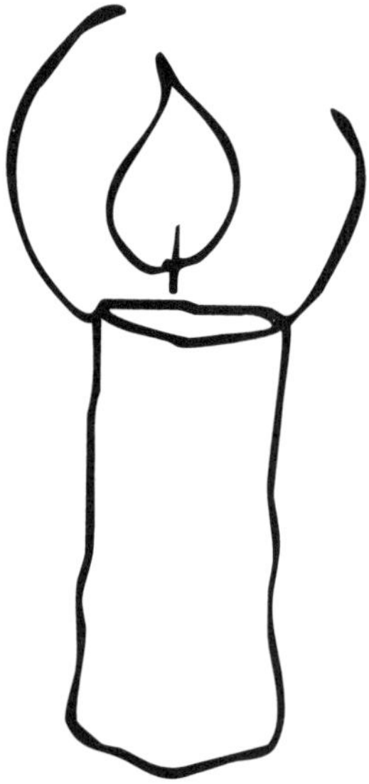

MANGER HOLIDAYS KING

SHEPHERDS WONDERLAND

WHAT DO YOU KNOW?

Jesus Is Born

When Jesus was born, Mary and Joseph were not at their home or even in their own city. Can you answer these questions about their journey to Bethlehem?

What powerful ruler said that everyone had to be registered in the cities where they were born? The answer is hidden in Luke 2:1.

_____

Mary and Joseph went to Bethlehem because Joseph was a descendant of what great king? The answer is hidden in Luke 2:4.

_____

Mary had her baby while they were on their trip. Why did she wrap up her new baby and lay Him in a manger filled with hay? The answer is hidden in Luke 2:7.

_____

PICTURE THIS

Draw a line from each picture to its matching word in the middle. When you are through, a few words will be left over. Fill them in on the lines below to form a phrase.

mistletoe

under

Christmas tree

baby Jesus

candle

bells

the

_____ _____ _____

THANKSGIVING SONGS

Find the missing words from the list below.

NOW THANK WE ALL OUR _____-

COME, YE THANKFUL _____ COME

WE GATHER _____

WITH _____ HEARTS, O LORD WE COME

COUNT YOUR _____

PEOPLE   BLESSINGS   GOD

TOGETHER   THANKFUL

WHAT DO YOU KNOW?

The Shepherds' Joy

On the night Jesus, the Christ Child, was born, some shepherds
were up in the hills taking care of their sheep. All of a sudden,
the sky lit up. Can you answer these questions?

Who appeared in the sky and told them not to be afraid?
The answer is hidden in Luke 2:9.

_____

The angel told the shepherds that a baby had been born.
What did the angel call the baby? The answer is hidden in Luke 2:11.

_____

The angels told the shepherds where they could find the baby Jesus.
Where did they say He would be lying?
The answer is hidden in Luke 2:12.

_____

WHAT DO YOU KNOW?

The Shepherds Find the Baby

When the angels finished their singing, the shepherds were filled
with joy. Can you answer these questions?

What did the shepherds do when the angels disappeared?
The answer is hidden in Luke 2:15.

_____

What did the shepherds do on their way home?
The answer is hidden in Luke 2:20.

_____

WHAT DO YOU KNOW?

Naming the Baby

Mary and Joseph did everything they could for their new baby.
Can you answer these questions?

When Jesus was eight days old, what did His parents name Him?
The answer is hidden in Luke 2:21.

_____

Where did Mary and Joseph take their new son a few days later?
The answer is hidden in Luke 2:22.

_____

What else did Mary and Joseph do while they were in Jerusalem?
The answer is hidden in Luke 2:24.

_____

GIVING THANKS

Fill in the missing letters to form a word or phrase from top to bottom.

```
        __ E A S T
    I N D __ A N S
        C __ A N B E R R I E S
          __ W E E T  P O T A T O E S
    S W E E __  C O R N
          __ U R K E Y
  P L Y M O U T __
          M __ Y F L O W E R
    B E A __  S
    P U M P __ I N  P I E
          __ T U F F I N G
      V E __ E T A B L E S
    F A M __ L Y
    H A R __ E S T
    S H A R __ N G
    A C O R __
      P I L __ R I M S
```

WHAT DO YOU KNOW?

Going to the Temple

Mary and Joseph made sure to dedicate Jesus to the Lord. Can you answer these questions?

Whom did Mary and Joseph meet in the Temple in Jerusalem?
The answer is hidden in Luke 2:25.

_____

What did Simeon do when he saw the baby Jesus?
The answer is hidden in Luke 2:28.

_____

Simeon told Mary and Joseph that Jesus would be great and save us all. What did they do when they heard these words?
The answer is hidden in Luke 2:33.

_____

Everyone Loves Snow

```
B  S  H  O  V  E  L  M
O  H  S  A  W  O  L  P
A  O  K  W  E  P  A  S
R  E  D  N  U  O  B  T
D  N  M  L  F  J  N  O
F  L  A  K  E  A  U  R
P  A  N  G  E  L  L  M
W  H  I  T  E  N  R  L
```

ball	flake	shovel
board	man	storm
bound	plow	angel
fall	shoe	white

THE HOLY BIRTH

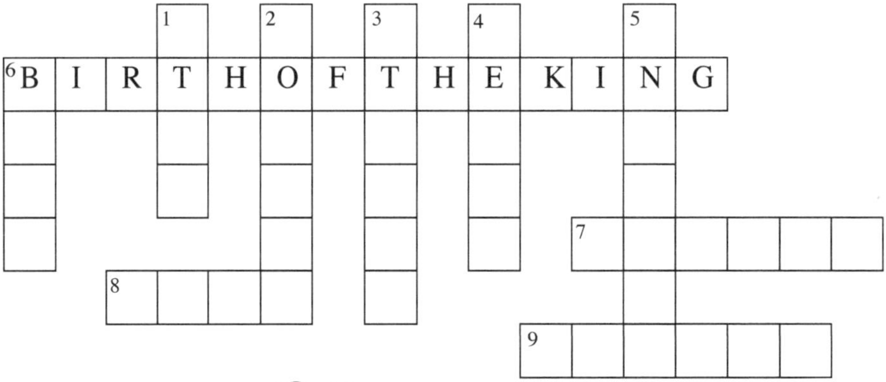
1
2
3
4
5
6 B I R T H O F T H E K I N G
7
8
9

ACROSS

7. This is where Mary placed the newborn king.
8. This is the name of Jesus' mother.
9. This is the name of Jesus' earthly father.

DOWN

1. The wise men followed a ___________.
2. Mary rode to Bethlehem on a ______________.
3. There were no rooms so the baby was born in a __________.
4. Mary and Joseph named the baby ______________.
5. There were ___________ in the stable.
6. The shepherds and wise men were looking for the ________.

WHAT DO YOU KNOW?

Also in the Temple

After Simeon blessed Jesus and told His parents about Him, they met a woman named Anna. Can you answer these questions?

How old was the woman Joseph and Mary met in the Temple?
The answer is hidden in Luke 2:37.

_____

What did this woman do all day? The answer is hidden in Luke 2:37.

_____

What did Anna do when she saw Jesus?
The answer is hidden in Luke 2:38.

_____

PICTURE THIS

Draw a line from each picture to its matching word in the middle. When you are through, a few words will be left over. Fill them in on the lines below to form a phrase.

God

snowman

Christmas tree

gingerbread house

bells

to   thanks

_____   _____   _____

HOLIDAY SONGS

Find the missing words from the list below.

IT'S THE MOST _____ TIME OF THE YEAR

WHAT _____ IS THIS?

GO TELL IT ON THE _____

DECK THE _____

JOY TO THE _____

CHILD HALLS WORLD

MOUNTAIN WONDERFUL

WHAT DO YOU KNOW?

Who Is Jesus?

Jesus, the Christ Child, is the most important person in all the Bible. Long before He was born, God told people about Him. Can you answer these questions?

What name did God give to Jesus?
The answer is hidden in Isaiah 7:14.

_____

What does the Bible say will be upon Jesus' shoulders?
The answer is hidden in Isaiah 9:6.

_____

What tribe or clan does the Bible say Jesus will come from?
The answer is hidden in Micah 5:2.

_____

Staying Warm

```
B  H  E  A  T  D  F  H
L  S  T  K  I  O  L  O
A  E  H  E  C  O  A  T
N  C  R  C  F  W  N  C
K  E  O  H  N  E  N  O
E  E  W  D  G  R  E  C
T  L  I  U  Q  I  L  O
M  F  E  R  I  F  N  A
```

blanket   fleece   throw
quilt   firewood   coat
flannel   heat   hot cocoa

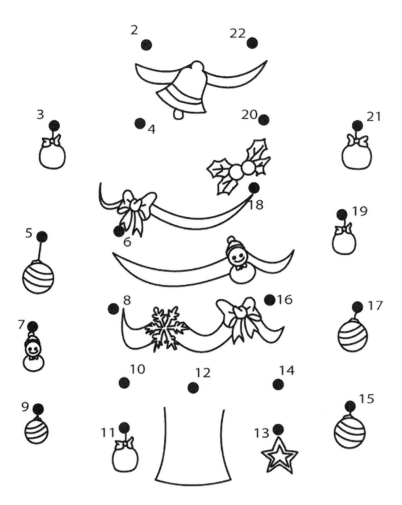

THE ANGELS' SONG

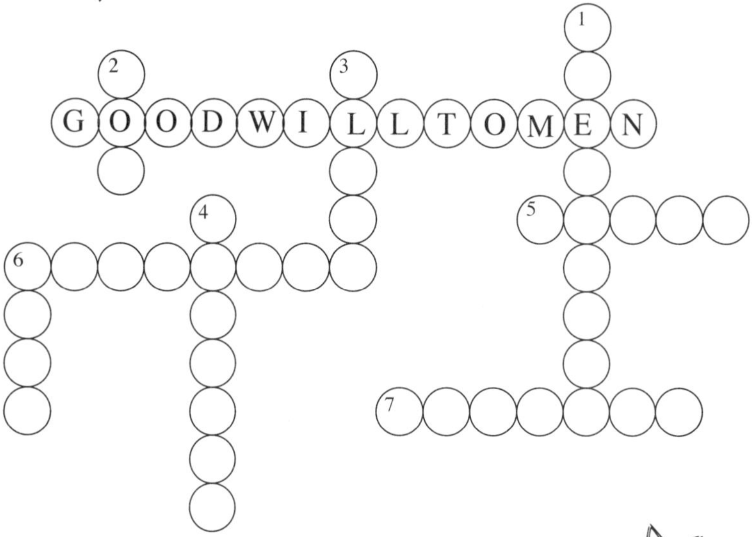

GOODWILLTOMEN

ACROSS

5. The shepherds take care of the _____.
6. The angels were called the _____ host.
7. The angels sang _____ to God.

DOWN

1. The sheep are cared for by the _____.
2. The angels brought tidings of great _____.
3. The _____ of the Lord shone round about the angels.
4. The angels told the shepherds to _____.
6. The angels were called the heavenly _____.

WHAT DO YOU KNOW?

The Christ Child

Can you answer these questions about the Christ Child?

Long before Jesus was born, God gave Him many titles.
Can you name any of them hidden in Isaiah 9:6?

_____

_____

_____

_____

_____

When will God's Kingdom end? The answer is hidden in Isaiah 9:7.

_____

WHAT DO YOU KNOW?

The Three Kings

Can you answer these questions about the three kings who came to visit the Christ Child?

These kings came to Jerusalem from far away in the East. How did they find their way? The answer is hidden in Matthew 2:2.

_____

What did the three kings do when they found Jesus? The answer is hidden in Matthew 2:11.

_____

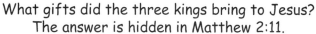

What gifts did the three kings bring to Jesus? The answer is hidden in Matthew 2:11.

_____

HOLIDAY CHEER

C	A	M	E	L	S	A	N	D	C	A	N	D	L	E	S

ACROSS

6. The First _____.

8. The songs we sing at Christmas are called _____.

DOWN

1. We like to ring these at Christmas.

2. We sign and send these to our friends at Christmas.

3. A time of prayer during the holidays.

4. Mary laid Jesus in a _____ bed.

5. We love to bake all kinds of these at Christmas.

7. We wrap these around the tree and turn them on.

PICTURE THIS

Draw a line from each picture to its matching word in the middle. When you are through, a few words will be left over. Fill them in on the lines below to form a phrase.

camel

bells

Mary

and

Joseph

baby Jesus

angel

_____ ____ _____

HOLIDAY SONGS

Find the missing words from the list below.

IT'S BEGINNING TO _____ A LOT LIKE CHRISTMAS

I _____ THE BELLS ON CHRISTMAS DAY

LITTLE _____ BOY

_____ NAVIDAD

O _____ TREE

DRUMMER   FELIZ   CHRISTMAS

HEARD   LOOK

WHAT DO YOU KNOW?

Winter in the Bible

The Bible has a lot to say about wintertime.
Can you answer these questions?

What is as refreshing as a faithful messenger?
The answer is hidden in Proverbs 25:13.

_____

What is it like when someone promises you a gift but doesn't give it
to you? The answer is hidden in Proverbs 25:14.

_____

What is it like when you sing a cheerful song to someone who is sad?
The answer is hidden in Proverbs 25:20.

_____

WHAT DO YOU KNOW?

Winter in the Bible

The Bible has a lot to say about wintertime.
Can you answer these questions?

The Bible says that the "coming of refreshing rain in winter" is like
what? The answer is hidden in Hosea 6:3.

_____

The Bible says the "cold" comes from where?
The answer is hidden in Job 37:9.

_____

The Bible says "ice" comes from where?
The answer is hidden in Job 37:10.

_____

Help "T" to find the rest of his word. . .TURKEY.

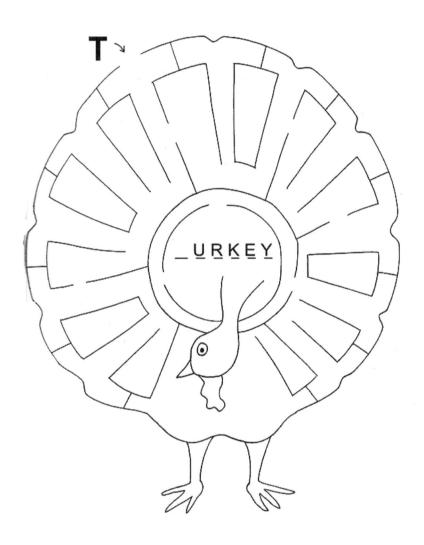

MARY'S MIRACLE

Fill in the missing letters, and the circled letters
will form a word or phrase from top to bottom.

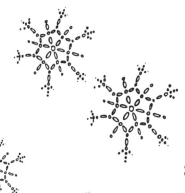

JE◯US

NAT◯VITY

ANGE◯S

SHEPH◯RDS

DO◯KEY

S◯AR

A◯IMALS

K◯NG OF KINGS

MAN◯ER

JOSEP◯

BIR◯H

HOLIDAY SONGS

Find the missing words from the list below.

HAVE YOURSELF A _____ LITTLE CHRISTMAS

_____ WE HAVE HEARD ON HIGH

GOD _____ YE MERRY GENTLEMEN

O COME ALL YE _____

THE _____ NOEL

FIRST   REST   FAITHFUL

MERRY   ANGELS

WHAT DO YOU KNOW?

Winter in the Bible

The apostle Paul was arrested and sent to Rome on a ship where he would be put on trial. High winds and winter storms made the trip very dangerous. Can you answer these questions about Paul's winter journey?

Where did the ship finally stop?
The answer is hidden in Acts 27:7-8.

_____

When they left Fair Havens, Paul's ship set sail for what harbor in Crete? The answer is hidden in Acts 27:12.

_____

Everyone was afraid when the ship started to sink. What did Paul tell the frightened men who were on the ship with him? The answer is hidden in Acts 27:22.

_____

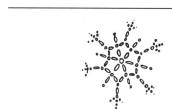

JOSEPH'S JOURNEY

Fill in the missing letters, and the circled letters
will form a word or phrase from top to bottom.

__ A G I

__ G Y P T

H E __ O D

N O __ O O M

D O N K E __

C H R I S T __ H I L D

S __ E P H E R D S

M A __ Y

B __ R T H

A N G E L __

S __ A R

E __ M A N U E L

N __ T I V I T Y

J E __ U S

PICTURE THIS

Draw a line from each picture to its matching word in the middle. When you are through, a few words will be left over. Fill them in on the lines below to form a phrase.

holiday bells

Christmas tree

and

bows

boxes

turkey

dove

_____ ____ ____ _____

WHAT DO YOU KNOW?

Winter in the Bible

The wind can be very cold in the wintertime.
Can you answer these questions about the wind?

When the winter winds and rain beat against the house built
on the rock, did it fall or did it stand strong?
The answer is hidden in Matthew 7:25.

_____

When the tall waves and winter wind started to sink the boat Jesus
and His disciples were sailing in, Jesus stood up and spoke to the
storm. What did Jesus say? The answer is hidden in Mark 4:37–39.

_____

Where does the Bible say that God walks?
The answer is hidden in Psalm 104:3.

_____

ALL THE WAY

Fill in the missing letters to form
a word or phrase from top to bottom.

_ O L L Y

R I N G _ N G

S _ O W

S L E I _ H

_ I G H T S

O N _ H O R S E

_ O B T A I L

O P _ N

_ A U G H T E R

F I E _ D S

_ O N G S

PICTURE THIS

Draw a line from each picture to its matching word in the middle. When you are through, a few words will be left over. Fill them in on the lines below to form a phrase.

snowflake

holly   tree

the

gifts

toys

under

wise men

_____ _____ _____ _____

WHAT DO YOU KNOW?

Winter in the Bible

The Bible has a lot to say about wintertime.
Can you answer these questions?

The Bible names five kinds of "weather." Can you name them?
The answer is hidden in Psalm 148:8.

_____

_____

_____

_____

_____

What did all these types of weather do?
The answer is hidden in Psalm 148:8.

_____

STORMY WEATHER

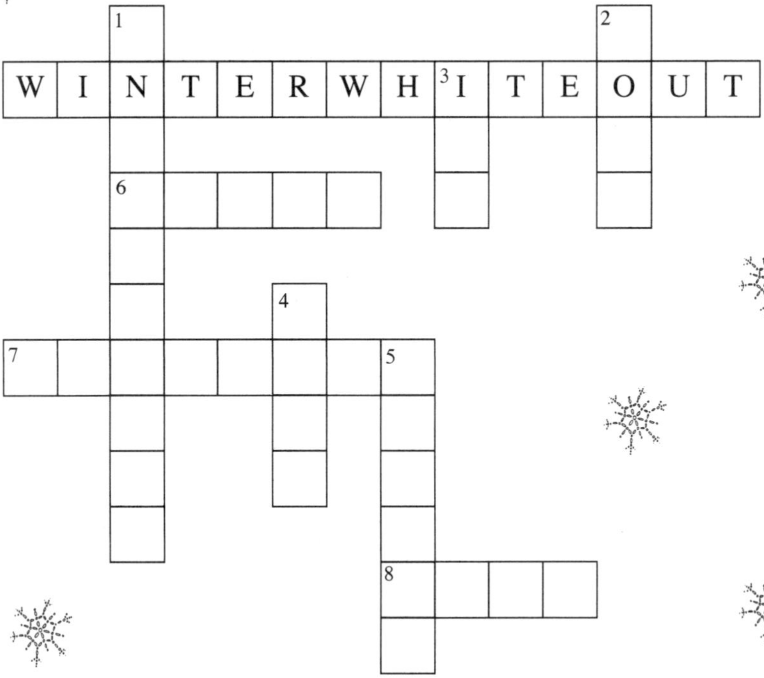

ACROSS

6. When the trees and the clouds are moving, it's _________.
7. A really bad snowstorm is called a ____________.
8. Water from the clouds is called ___________.

DOWN

1. The snow piles up and makes ______________.
2. Winter winds blow in ____________ air.
3. In winter the roads can get ______________.
4. When rain freezes into hard chunks, we call it _________.
5. Stormy weather can be very ___________.

WHAT DO YOU KNOW?

Winter in the Bible

The Bible uses snow to describe the whitest white of all. Can you answer these questions about things that are "as white as snow"?

What does the Bible say was "white as snow"?
The answer is hidden in Daniel 7:9.

_____

What does the Bible say shall be as "white as snow"?
The answer is hidden in Isaiah 1:18.

_____

What does the Bible say God will do to make us "whiter than snow"?
The answer is hidden in Psalm 51:7.

_____

FAMILY FUN

T	R	I	M	M	I	N	G	T	H	E	T	R	E	E

ACROSS

6. Striped candy with a hook, these are candy _____.
7. There are jingle _____ and silver _____.
8. These are made with brightly colored ribbon.

DOWN

1. This goes on top of the tree.
2. These are shiny strips of paper to brighten the tree.
3. These comes in all colors and flash off and on.
4. These are under the tree to be opened on Christmas Day.
5. These come in many shapes, colors, and sizes.

238

PICTURE THIS

Draw a line from each picture to its matching word in the middle. When you are through, a few words will be left over. Fill them in on the lines below to form a phrase.

drum

candle

the

wrap

gifts

stocking

mittens

_____ _____ _____

WHAT DO YOU KNOW?

Winter in the Bible

The Bible has a lot to say about wintertime.
Can you answer these questions?

The Bible says the "snow" is like what?
The answer is hidden in Psalm 147:16.

_____

In the same psalm, the Bible says the "frost" is like what?
The answer is hidden in Psalm 147:16.

_____

What is it God says to the "snow"? The answer is hidden in Job 37:6.

_____

Winter Birds

```
B L A C K A R T
B I R D S B O H
L F E T P L B R
U I V S A U I U
E N O W R E N S
J C D A R T L H
A H W M O I F E
Y S R W W T O S
```

black	wrens	robin
bird	finch	bluetit
bluejay	thrushes	sparrow
	dove	

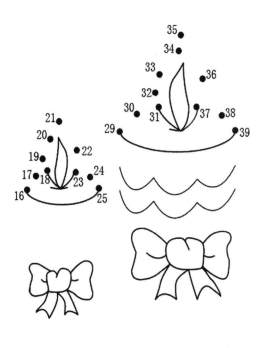

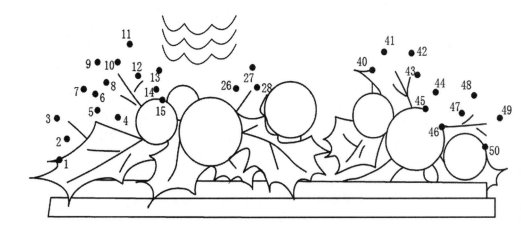

HOLIDAY GREETINGS

Find the missing words from the list below.

CHRISTMAS IS FOR _____

THE CHRISTMAS _____ IS A GIVING HEART

GOOD _____ OF GREAT JOY

JESUS IS THE _____ FOR THE SEASON

THE JOY OF CHRISTMAS BRINGS US _____ TO EACH OTHER

GOD _____ US EVERYONE

BLESS   TIDINGS   CLOSER

HEART   CHILDREN   REASON

WHAT DO YOU KNOW?

Winter in the Bible

The Bible says that God is the only one who can control the weather.
He decides when it will be cold and when it will be warm.
Can you answer these questions?

What does the Bible say only God can do?
The answer is hidden in Job 37:3.

_____

What does the Bible say only God can call down from heaven?
The answer is hidden in Job 37:6.

_____

What is it the Bible says God's people are safe from even
when this kind of weather comes down on them?
The answer is hidden in Isaiah 32:18–19.

_____

WHAT DO YOU KNOW?

Winter in the Bible

The wind and weather are no problem for God.
Can you answer these questions?

What does the Bible say God rode on when He flew upon the wings of the wind? The answer is hidden in Psalm 18:10.

_____

The Bible says that dark waters and what other kind of weather was round about God? The answer is hidden in Psalm 18:11.

_____

What does the Bible say God did in the heavens?
The answer is hidden in Psalm 18:13.

_____

Journey of the Magi!

```
T  S  A  E  Z  Y  S  O
H  R  R  Y  M  R  T  S
R  E  M  N  D  O  A  T
E  M  R  S  Y  L  R  F
E  D  L  U  G  G  O  I
Y  B  A  B  D  N  A  G
S  L  E  M  A  C  I  O
S  T  A  B  L  E  M  K
```

camels	baby	gold
three	east	stable
kings	myrrh	gifts
	star	

KINGLY GIFTS

Fill in the missing letters to form a word or phrase from top to bottom.

P __ A Y

K __ N G

B E __ H L E H E M

G I F __ S

S M I __ E D

B __ S T

__ R U M

H O N O __

P A R __ M

P U __ P U M

__ A G I

J __ S U S

P __ A I S E

L A M __

S __ N G

B A B __

WHAT DO YOU KNOW?

Winter in the Bible

The Bible has a lot to say about wintertime.
Can you answer these questions?

Where do the "snow and rain" come from?
The answer is hidden in Isaiah 55:10.

_____

How do the "rain and snow" make the earth better?
The answer is hidden in Isaiah 55:10.

_____

_____

_____

What does the Bible say is like the "rain and snow"?
The answer is hidden in Isaiah 55:11.

_____

Unscramble the Bold Letters in the Poem to Answer the Question

Whose birthday do we celebrate each Christmas?

M**e**rry Christmas to everyone;
God **s**ent His one and only Son.
Just a baby born one starry night,
His mother Mary wrapped Him tight.
Shepherds came from field**s** to see
Who the promised King wo**u**ld be.

As you celebrate Christmas this year,
Remember _ _ _ _ _ loves you dear.

FROM THE EAST

Fill in the missing letters to form a word
or phrase from top to bottom.

◯ORSHIP

CAM◯LS

ROYAL◯Y

◯OLY

MYR◯H

H◯ROD

J◯SUS

SEE◯

G◯FTS

FRA◯KINCENSE

◯OLD

◯TAR

WHAT DO YOU KNOW?

Who Is the Messiah?

Joseph and Mary named their first child Jesus. They knew
He was special because God had sent angels to tell them all
they needed to know. They could hardly believe that their little
boy was the Messiah—the One who would save the people of
Israel from their captors. Can you answer these questions
about Jesus the Messiah from Matthew 1:1–17?

What two great people were Jesus the Messiah's ancestors?
The answer is hidden in Matthew 1:1.

_____

What tribe of Israel was Jesus descended from?
The answer is hidden in Matthew 1:3.

_____

Who was the father of Joseph, the husband of Mary,
who was Jesus' mother? The answer is hidden in Matthew 1:16.

_____

How many generations were there between Abraham and King David?
The answer is hidden in Matthew 1:17.

_____

Eyewitnesses to the Birth

```
A  N  N  A  Z  T  D  C
C  L  H  P  E  S  O  J
L  E  A  N  L  O  N  F
J  O  Y  E  I  H  K  O
K  N  G  S  H  E  E  P
W  N  R  M  A  R  Y  N
A  E  L  B  A  T  S  L
D  R  E  H  P  E  H  S
```

shepherd	angels	sheep
Anna	Mary	stable
donkeys	Joseph	hay
	joy	

Celebrating the Letter *T*

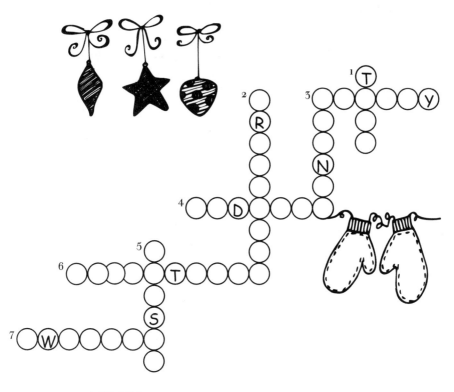

ACROSS

3. It's on the holiday menu.
4. The angels brought good _____ of great joy.
6. They are passed down to us.
7. The lights on the tree and the stars in the sky do this.

DOWN

1. Where the ornaments go.
2. Christmas dinner with all the _____.
3. Our greatest gift to God.
5. It sparkles on the tree.

HOLY FAMILY

Fill in the missing letters to form a word or phrase from top to bottom.

BE __ H L E H E M

J O S E P __

J __ S U S

D O __ K E Y

M __ R Y

B I R __ H

__ N N K E E P E R

T R A __ E L

A N __ M A L S

__ A X E S

E G __ P T

Holiday Stories

Find the missing words from the list below.

MRS. BROWNLOW'S CHRISTMAS _____

HARRY THE SINGING _____

NO CRIB FOR A _____

THE GIFT OF THE _____

A CHRISTMAS _____ AND HOW IT CAME TRUE

ANGEL   BED   DREAM
MAGI   PARTY

WHAT DO YOU KNOW?

The Birth of Jesus the Messiah

The Bible tells us all about the day Jesus was born.
Can you answer these questions about
the birth of Jesus the Messiah?

Mary was engaged to be married to Joseph, but
someone else was Jesus' real father. Who was it?
The answer is hidden in Matthew 1:18.

_____

Who told Joseph all about God's plan to bring Jesus into the world?
The answer is hidden in Matthew 1:20.

_____

What did the angel tell Joseph?
The answer is hidden in Matthew 1:20.

_____

What did the angel tell Joseph to name Mary's child?
The answer is hidden in Matthew 1:21.

_____

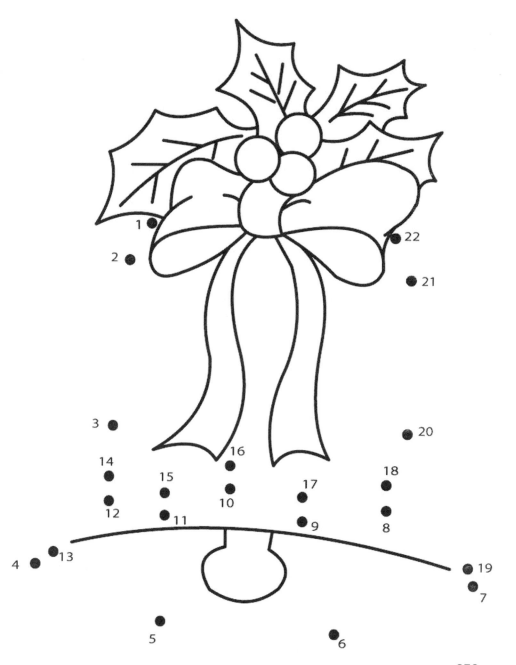

259

Celebrating the letter *H*

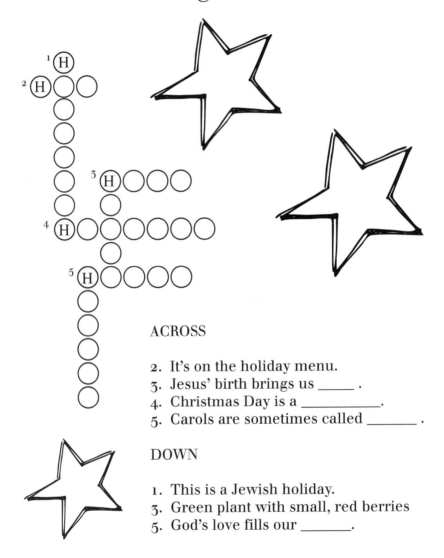

ACROSS

2. It's on the holiday menu.
3. Jesus' birth brings us _____ .
4. Christmas Day is a _____.
5. Carols are sometimes called _____ .

DOWN

1. This is a Jewish holiday.
3. Green plant with small, red berries
5. God's love fills our _____.

How Many Words Can You Make from the Letters in

SNOWFLAKES?

_____   _____

_____   _____

_____   _____

_____   _____

_____   _____

_____   _____

_____   _____

_____   _____

_____   _____

WHAT DO YOU KNOW?

Journey of the Wise Men

The Magi, also known as the Wise Men and the
Three Kings, came looking for the Christ Child.
Can you answer these questions?

What question did the Wise Men ask when they arrived in
Jerusalem? The answer is hidden in Matthew 2:2.

_____

What special sign had they followed from their homes faraway in
the East? The answer is hidden in Matthew 2:2.

_____

What did they wish to do when they found the Christ Child?
The answer is hidden in Matthew 2:2.

_____

WHAT DO YOU KNOW?

Herod's Evil Plan

When King Herod heard that some kings from the East
were looking for the Christ Child, he was angry and disturbed.
Can you answer these questions?

Who did Herod call on to tell him about the Christ Child?
The answer is hidden in Matthew 2:4.

_____

What did these advisors tell King Herod about where the Christ
Child would be born? The answer is hidden in Matthew 2:5.

_____

What did the advisors tell King Herod about what the Christ Child
would do? The answer is hidden in Matthew 2:6.

_____

Can you find your way
from the base of the
Christmas tree all the
way to the star?

WHAT DO YOU KNOW?

Herod Meets the Wise Men

King Herod was not happy when he heard who the Wise Men were looking for and why. Can you answer these questions?

King Herod sent the Wise Men a secret message to come see him. What did he ask them? The answer is hidden in Matthew 2:7.

_____

What did King Herod do when he finished talking to the Wise Men? The answer is hidden in Matthew 2:8.

_____

What did he ask the Wise Men to do for him? The answer is hidden in Matthew 2:8.

_____

Songs for the Season

```
H   J   A   N   J   O   Y   M
F   I   R   S   T   S   A   A
M   N   O   E   L   I   W   N
E   G   Y   I   F   L   A   G
D   L   R   O   W   E   R   E
B   E   L   L   S   N   A   R
J   N   I   G   H   T   T   G
R   E   D   N   O   W   S   P
```

jingle	silent	star
bells	night	wonder
away	joy	first
manger	world	noel

Match the Gifts
with Their Shadows

WHAT DO YOU KNOW?

The Wise Men Continue Their Journey

King Herod sent the Wise Men to find the Christ Child
and return to let him know when they found him.
Can you answer these questions?

How did the Wise Men find their way to Bethlehem?
The answer is hidden in Matthew 2:9.

_____

What did the Wise Men do when they found Mary and Child?
The answer is hidden in Matthew 2:11.

_____

What did the Wise Men bring for the Christ Child?
The answer is hidden in Matthew 2:11.

_____

The Wise Men did not return to King Herod. Who warned them?
The answer is hidden in Matthew 2:12.

_____

HOLIDAY FUN

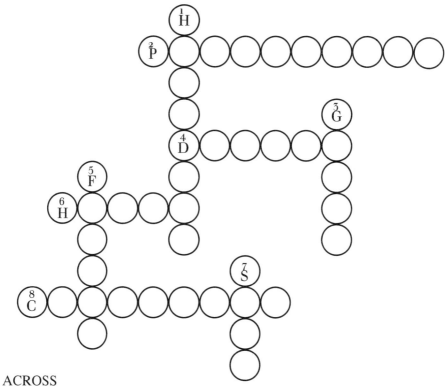

ACROSS

2. This red plant is a Christmas favorite.
4. The whole family gathers for this special meal.
6. The presents and fun make us _____.
8. Christmas is a time to _____.

DOWN

1. Thanksgiving, Christmas, and New Year are the _____.
3. Red and _____ are the colors of the season.
5. During the holidays, we love to get together with _____.
7. It blazed in the sky over the stable where Jesus was born.

Holy Night

Fill in the missing letters to form a word or phrase from top to bottom.

S __ E P H E R D S

FI __ L D S

PR __ I S E S

SA __ I O R

__ M M A N U E L

FEAR __ O T

ANGE __ S

CIT __ O F D A V I D

C __ R I S T

L __ R D

MES __ A G E

INFAN __

WHAT DO YOU KNOW?

Joseph Senses Danger

After the Wise Men had returned to the East,
Joseph wondered how he would keep his family safe.
Can you answer these questions?

Who appeared to Joseph in a dream?
The answer is hidden in Matthew 2:13.

_____

What did the angel instruct Joseph to do?
The answer is hidden in Matthew 2:13.

_____

What reason did the angel give?
The answer is hidden in Matthew 2:13.

_____

CELEBRATE THE SEASON

Fill in the missing letters to form a word or phrase from top to bottom.

CERE __ ONY

GATH __ RINGS

MEMO __ IES

SU __ PRISES

TO __ S

__ AROLERS

C __ ARITY

P __ ESENTS

L __ GHTS

__ HARING

__ REE

TRI __ MINGS

ST __ R

__ TOCKINGS

PICTURE THIS

Draw a line from each picture to its matching word in the middle. When you are through, a few words will be left over. Fill them in on the lines below to form a phrase.

shepherds

Christmas tree

Jesus

baby

gingerbread house

bells   the

_____   _____   _____

Help the Little Mouse Get
to the Christmas Star

Twinkle, Sparkle, Snowflakes Bright— Can You Find 8 Different Types

Celebrating Advent

```
S  E  L  D  N  A  C  H
W  S  O  N  G  S  R  A
R  D  V  B  M  A  G  I
E  C  E  E  N  I  P  S
A  J  P  A  X  Z  E  S
T  O  H  O  L  Y  A  E
H  Y  V  I  L  U  C  M
S  T  F  I  H  N  E  R
```

ivy	holy	peace
wreaths	magi	songs
joy	pine	candles
love	Messiah	

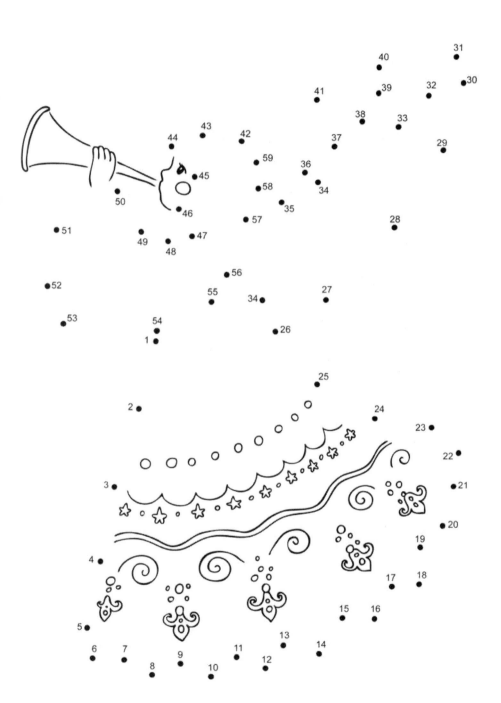

Reason for the Season

ACROSS

2. Jesus was born in a stable full of _____.
5. The baby's mother laid him in a _____.
6. Jesus' mother was _____ .
8. Jesus' earthly father was _____ .

DOWN

1. Mary rode into Bethlehem on a _____.
3. Mary gave birth to Jesus in a _____ .
4. Jesus was the long-awaited _____ .
7. There was __ _____ for the family in the inn.

WHAT DO YOU KNOW?

The Family Leaves Egypt

The Roman King Herod wanted to kill the baby Jesus.
But God told Joseph to take Him and His mother and
hide in Egypt. Can you answer these questions?

What happened to the terrible King Herod?
The answer is hidden in Matthew 2:19.

_____

How did Joseph know that it was safe to go home to Israel?
The answer is hidden in Matthew 2:19.

_____

What did the angel of the Lord tell Joseph?
The answer is hidden in Matthew 2:20.

_____

Christmas Candyland

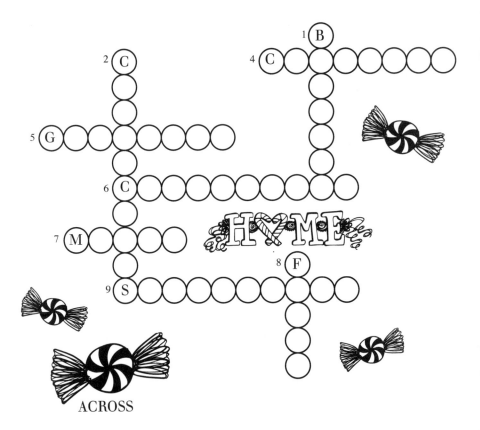

ACROSS

4. Firm, brown, chewy squares.
5. Sugar coated and made from gelatin.
6. A box of these make a great gift.
7. Spear____ or pepper____.
9. Round candy made from dried fruit.

DOWN

1. This candy is flat, hard, and has peanuts.
2. These have red stripes and a hook on the end.
8. Soft, creamy chocolate candy with pecans or walnuts.

PICTURE THIS

Draw a line from each picture to its matching word in the middle. When you are through, a few words will be left over. Fill them in on the lines below to form a phrase.

reindeer

angel

under

stocking

the

mistletoe

mittens

_____ ___ _____

Sharing Smiles and Good Cheer
Blesses People
All through the Year

List 10 Things That Make You Smile

The Blessed Nativity!

```
J  O  S  E  P  H  D  C
E  L  P  L  O  U  O  H
S  T  A  B  L  E  N  I
U  Y  B  Y  U  K  K  L
S  C  A  T  T  L  E  D
B  B  B  M  A  R  Y  B
E  W  Y  S  T  A  R  G
C  H  R  I  S  T  R  E
```

Joseph	baby	child
donkey	Jesus	star
Mary	stable	Christ
cattle		

287

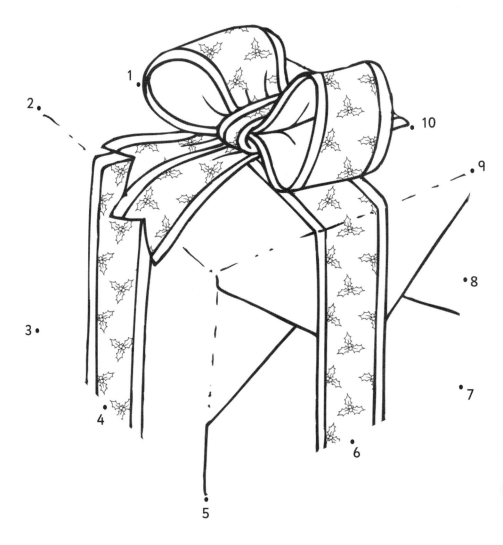

The Heavenly Host

ACROSS

2. God's creatures who watch over us.
3. The animals being watched by night.
6. The angels sang about peace,_____ toward men.
8. The angels sang _____ to God.

DOWN

1. These were watching over the sheep.
4. The angels brought good tidings of great _____.
5. The angels gave _____ to God.
7. The angels sang about _____ on earth.

PICTURE THIS

Draw a line from each picture to its matching word in the middle. When you are through, a few words will be left over. Fill them in on the lines below to form a phrase.

camel

bells

dream

of

Christmas tree

snow

angel

_____ ___ _____

WHAT DO YOU KNOW?

The Family Returns to Israel

As soon as Joseph heard that Herod was dead, he packed
up his family and went back home to Israel. Can you
answer thesequestions about their journey home?

On their way back to Israel, Joseph heard there was a new king.
Who was he? The answer is hidden in Matthew 2:22.

_____

How did God warn Joseph? The answer is hidden in Matthew 2:22.

_____

Where did Joseph, Mary, and the Christ Child go to stay safe?
The answer is hidden in Matthew 2:23.

_____

Holiday Pies!

```
M A E R C E C I
Q S B E R R Y S
R H U B A R B F
A T T S R L I N
P L R E I S S A
P I H C A E P C
L C R E A M L E
E N I K P M U P
```

ice cream	apple	cherry
peach	rhubarb	cream
pecan	berry	pumpkin

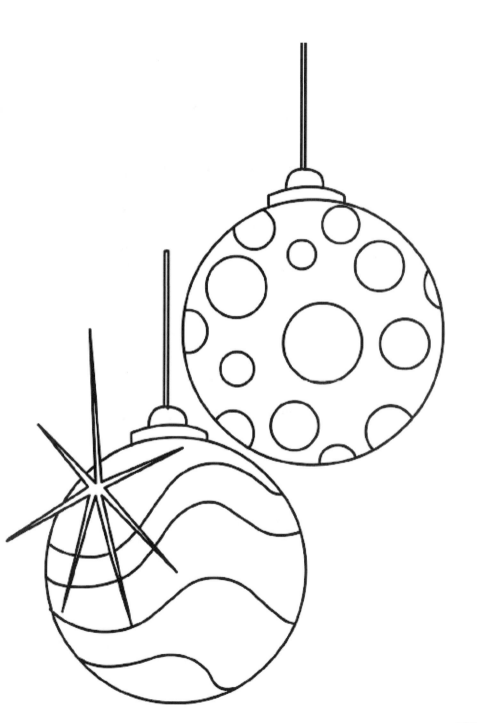

Boxes and Bows

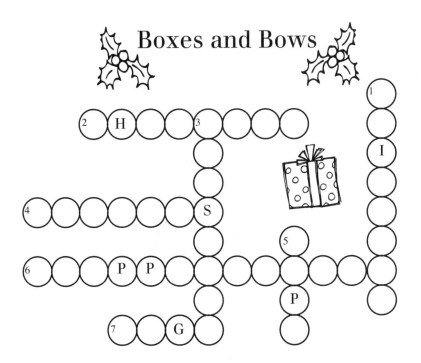

ACROSS

2. Rushing from store to store.
4. These make beautiful bows.
6. Put this around the gifts to keep them hidden.
7. These tell us who the gift is for.

DOWN

1. Use these to cut the paper.
3. Gifts are also called _____.
5. This sticky stuff keeps the paper in place.

WHAT DO YOU KNOW?

Winter in the Bible

The Bible has a lot to say about wintertime.
Can you answer these questions?

Who created summer and winter?
The answer is hidden in Psalm 74:17.

_____

What four things will never cease?
The answer is hidden in Genesis 8:22.

_____

_____

_____

_____

Christmas Joy!

```
K O T I N S E L
E T A R O C E D
M R L I G H T S
Y S T F I G O T
I B D R S C Y A
P Z Y T E B S N
C D A N G E L D
O R N A M E N T
```

tinsel   stand   ornament
decorate   gifts   tree
light   star   fir
    angel

Find These Things
You Would See in a Stable—
Each Word Is Hidden 2 Times

Hay • Manger • Cow • Sheep • Chicken • Donkey

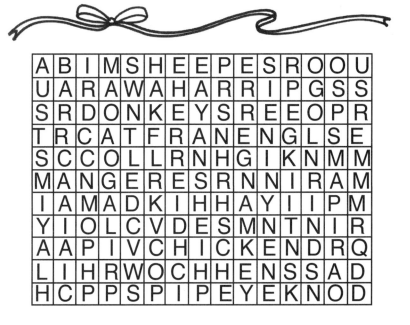

A	B	I	M	S	H	E	E	P	E	S	R	O	O	U
U	A	R	A	W	A	H	A	R	R	I	P	G	S	S
S	R	D	O	N	K	E	Y	S	R	E	E	O	P	R
T	R	C	A	T	F	R	A	N	E	N	G	L	S	E
S	C	C	O	L	L	R	N	H	G	I	K	N	M	M
M	A	N	G	E	R	E	S	R	N	N	I	R	A	M
I	A	M	A	D	K	I	H	H	A	Y	I	I	P	M
Y	I	O	L	C	V	D	E	S	M	N	T	N	I	R
A	A	P	I	V	C	H	I	C	K	E	N	D	R	Q
L	I	H	R	W	O	C	H	H	E	N	S	S	A	D
H	C	P	P	S	P	I	P	E	Y	E	K	N	O	D

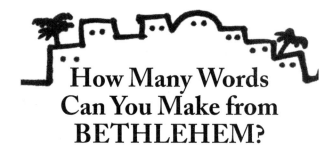

How Many Words Can You Make from BETHLEHEM?

_____   _____

_____   _____

_____   _____

_____   _____

_____   _____

_____   _____

_____   _____

_____   _____

_____   _____

Christmas Colors Are
RED & GREEN

Have an adult set a timer for 3 minutes. Ready, set, go—
list as many red and green things as you
can see around the room.

_____   _____

_____   _____

_____   _____

_____   _____

_____   _____

_____   _____

_____   _____

_____   _____

_____   _____

Celebrating the Letter *W*

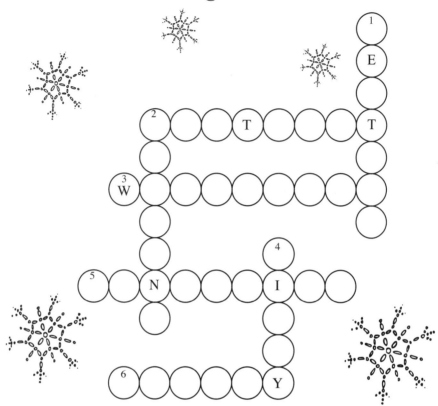

ACROSS
2. Another word for blizzard.
3. When you feed it, it fills the room with warmth.
5. How cold it is when the wind is blowing.
6. Snow and sleet are _____ weather.

DOWN
1. In winter, we must watch the _____.
2. What you would wear to stay warm.
4. The cold feels even colder when it's _____.

PICTURE THIS

Draw a line from each picture to its matching word in the middle. When you are through, a few words will be left over. Fill them in on the lines below to form a phrase.

holiday bells

Christmas tree

is

born

Jesus

present

stocking

_____ ___ _____

O Christmas Tree!

```
A N G E L L S G
R A T S Y O T I
B G I N T S A F
O R N A M E N T
K F S M Z W D S
Z E E R T R I F
G H L I G H T S
E T A R O C E D
```

tinsel   decorate   star
gifts   lights   angel
stand   ornament   fir tree
toys

PICTURE THIS

Draw a line from each picture to its matching word in the middle. When you are
through, a few words will be left over. Fill them in on the lines below to form a phrase.

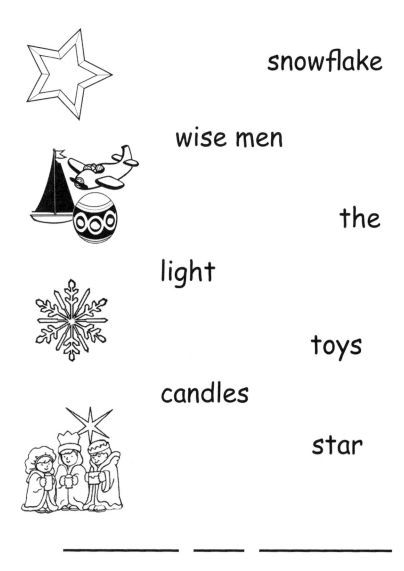

snowflake

wise men

the

light

toys

candles

star

_____ _____ _____

You will need a friend to play
this one. Take turns connecting
the dots. Whoever finishes the square
puts their initial in the
box. The person with the most
squares at the end wins.

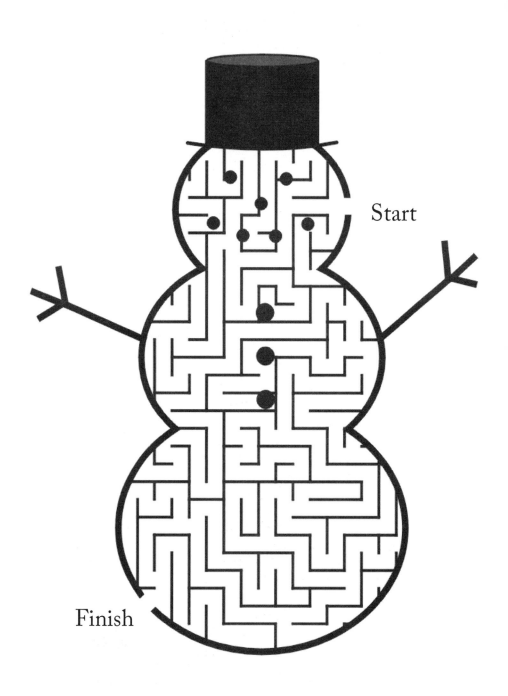

Start

Finish

Thanksgiving Grace

ACROSS
3. Where the Pilgrims landed.
4. The Pilgrims and Indians shared a _____.
5. The _____ showed the Pilgrims how to grow corn.
6. Thanksgiving is meant to celebrate the _____.
8. On Thanksgiving, we usually roast a _____.

DOWN
1. The _____ learned from the Indians.
2. The month in which we celebrate Thanksgiving.
7. The purpose of this holiday is to give _____.

Winter Sport Word Search

Find the winter sports that are listed below.

```
G B W P C T B L N Z F G G R Y
M N Q P R D K N T R N T N U F
B T I C E F I S H I N G I S I
W O T T E Y K G L S L L D L P
N X B O A E E I A M Q W R E V
Z N N S L K B K E Z Q Z A D L
R N Q E L O S X C J H X O D V
R G T N M E P E U O X A B I E
F O T W N G I S R P H V W N T
N R O Y H U G G Y U Y A O G Z
G N R Y A L Z L H H G O N Z W
S B G W K B S M X T F I S N N
U S P W K F H J J E U W F C J
K S V U Q Q H A L G N I I K S
H O Q L X C C X C C T N B A W
```

skiing	snowmobiling	sledding
ice fishing	figure skating	luge
snowboarding	hockey	bobsleigh

One is different in each row.
Circle the one that is different.

1.

2.

3.

The Shepherds' Glory!

```
H  P  W  K  S  T  A  R
O  E  F  I  E  L  D  E
S  E  A  L  C  J  L  G
T  H  N  V  A  O  I  N
H  S  G  E  E  Y  H  A
G  N  E  S  P  N  C  M
I  M  L  N  O  E  L  Q
N  T  S  I  R  H  C  Y
```

heavenly   night   angels
host   Christ   joy
field   child   noel
manger   sheep

Snow Snow Snow

ACROSS
2. A blizzard.
3. A round handful of snow.
4. It pushes the snow out of the street.
6. Snowy ice crystals.
7. A snowy creation with a carrot nose.
8. A big pile of snow.

DOWN
1. This is used to scoop the snow.
5. This is used to walk on snow.

PICTURE THIS

Draw a line from each picture to its matching word in the middle. When you are through, a few words will be left over. Fill them in on the lines below to form a phrase.

in

drum

ice skate

the

no

inn

hot chocolate

room

mittens

_____ _____ _____ _____ _____

Winter Sports Sudoku

There's no math involved. Each picture must be in the row (horizontal), the column (vertical), and the square. No picture can be used twice in the same row, column, or square. Draw the sledder that fits in the empty boxes.

Celebrating the letter *G*

ACROSS
2. A cake made with molasses and ginger.
5. Season's _____.
7. During the holidays, we exchange _____.

DOWN

1. Rope of flowers, greens, or tinsel.
2. A kindly feeling.
3. A string of greenery.
4. Those who visit our homes are _____.
6. A Dr. Seuss character.

Mother and Child

Fill in the missing letters, and the circled letters will
form a word or phrase from top to bottom.

GOD'S ◯ON

VIRG ◯N

ANGE ◯S

SHEPH ◯RDS

MA ◯GER

NA ◯IVITY

◯OEL

K ◯NG

MA ◯I

◯OPE

MAJES ◯Y

316

PICTURE THIS

Draw a line from each picture to its matching word in the middle. When you are through, a few words will be left over. Fill them in on the lines below to form a phrase.

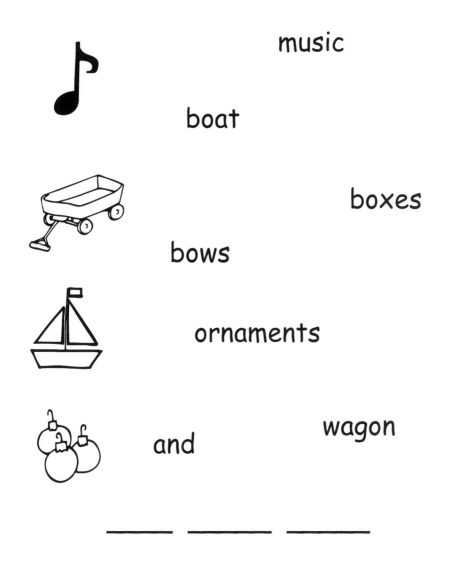

music

boat

boxes

bows

ornaments

and

wagon

_____ _____ _____

Tic-Tac-Toe

Circle the One That Is Different

The Angels' Glory

```
G N I S I A R P
L S O B N W N I
M P O N H I G H
H E A V E N L Y
O A D K K G O D
S C R V N S R L
T E S H O L Y T
G A B R I E L W
```

heavenly	on high	God
host	Gabriel	peace
praising	wings	holy

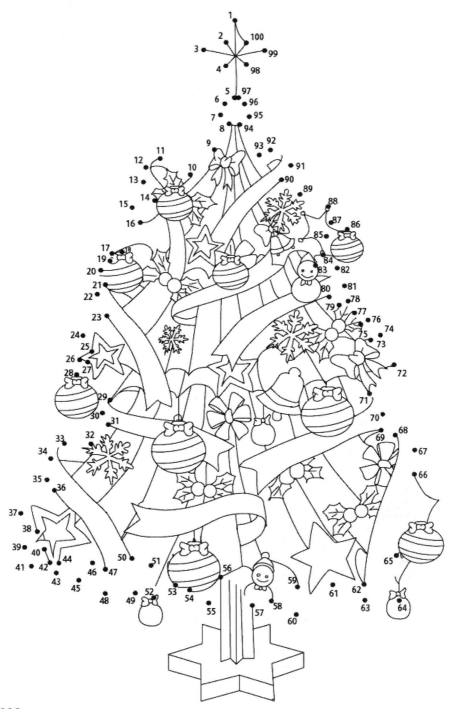

Surviving Winter

Fill in the missing letters, and the circled letters
will form a word or phrase from top to bottom.

◯CARVES

SWEA◯ERS

H◯TS

SUNN◯ DAYS

F◯REPLACE

LO◯G JOHNS

LEG◯INGS

◯OODSTOVE

BL◯NKETS

EA◯MUFFS

◯ITTENS

Find 7 Hearts in This Picture

*You will seek me and find me when
you seek me with all your heart.*
JEREMIAH 29:13 NIV

What's Different?

Start

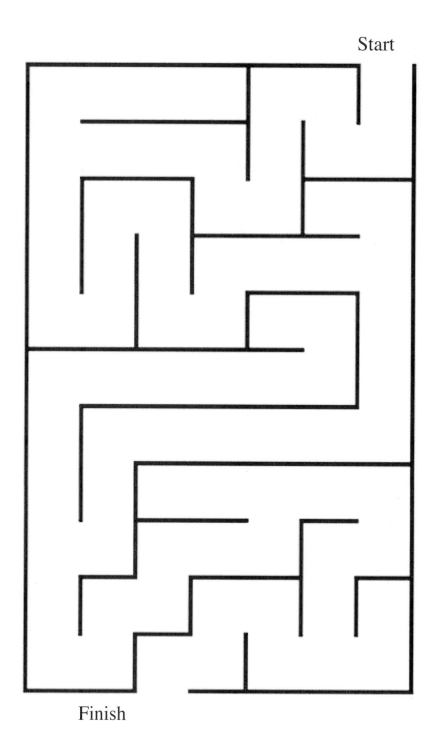

Finish

That Jolly Fellow

Fill in the missing letters, and the circled letters will
form a word or phrase from top to bottom.

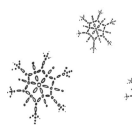

◯OME

C◯ROLING

◯ARTIES

GIFTWRA◯

CAND◯

C◯ARITY

GREAT F◯OD

MIST◯ETOE

TRAD◯TIONS

LIGHT ◯ISPLAYS

C◯RDS

FAMIL◯

◯HOPPING

Four in a Row

Grab a friend and take turns marking squares. The first to get 4 in a row vertically, horizontally, or diagonally wins.

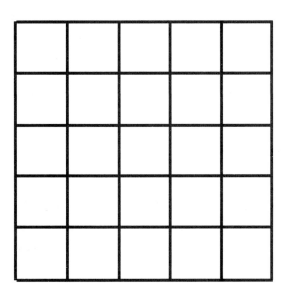

Christmas Tic-Tac-Toe

Write a Letter

to a friend or family member telling
them how much you love them.

Follow the Path

Write the number of the path in the box below.

You will need a friend to play this one. Take turns connecting the dots. Whoever finishes the square puts their initial in the box. The person with the most squares at the end wins.

Crossword

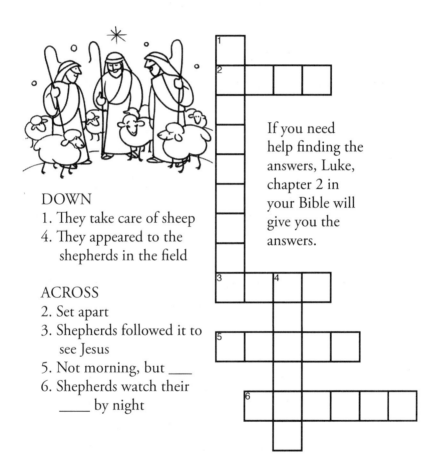

DOWN
1. They take care of sheep
4. They appeared to the
   shepherds in the field

ACROSS
2. Set apart
3. Shepherds followed it to
   see Jesus
5. Not morning, but ___
6. Shepherds watch their
   ____ by night

If you need
help finding the
answers, Luke,
chapter 2 in
your Bible will
give you the
answers.

Color Me

Find Your Way
through the Maze

Start Finish

Find Your Way
through the Maze

start

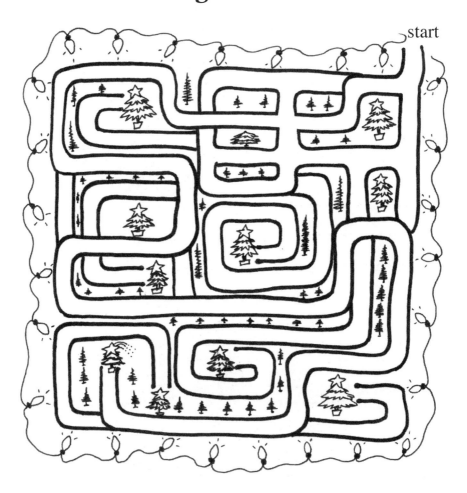

Crossword

ACROSS
1. Their coat is made of wool
3. It's what Mary rode on to Bethlehem
5. Jesus' mother's name

DOWN
2. Mary laid the baby in it
4. Town Jesus was born in

Tic-Tac-Toe

Color Me

How Many Words Can You Make from the Words CHRISTMAS GIFTS?

Decorate the Christmas Tree

Find Your Way through the Maze.
There Are Two Paths.

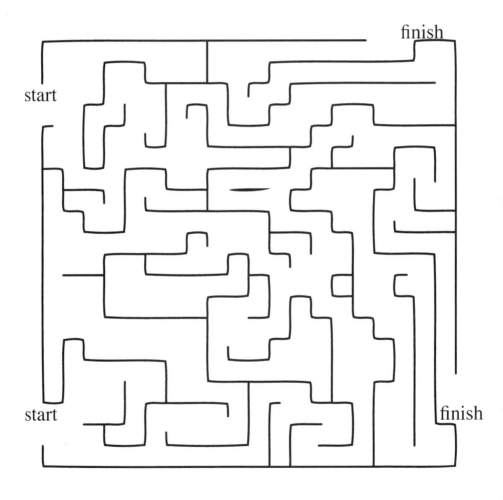

start

finish

start

finish

Each Year We Celebrate
Jesus' Birthday on Christmas.

As you color this cake, sing "Happy Birthday" to Jesus.

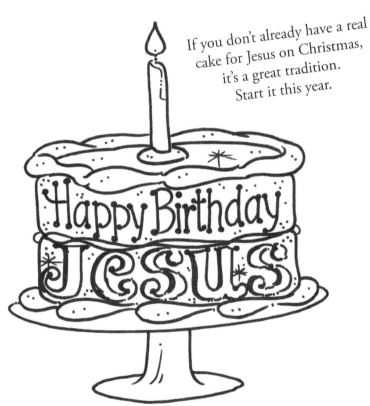

If you don't already have a real
cake for Jesus on Christmas,
it's a great tradition.
Start it this year.

Which One Is Different?

Happy Birthday,
Baby Jesus!

Christmas is the day we celebrate Jesus' birthday!
We can have fun with Santa Claus, but just don't forget the real
reason for the season! Celebrate Jesus this Christmas!

Write Your Own Christmas Song

Use some of the words provided to help you.

love, faith,
hope, snow,
bells, gifts,
travel, family,
world, coat,
sleigh, bundle,
skates, skiing,
cookies, candy,
Christmas,
heavenly

_____

_____

_____

_____

_____

_____

_____

_____

_____

_____

Follow the Path

Write the number of the path in the box below.

Help the Snowman Catch
SNOWFLAKES

Catch the letters and unscramble them on the line
below to get the snowman's message to you.

_ _ _ _ _   _ _ _ _ _   _ _ _!

Circle the One
That Is Different

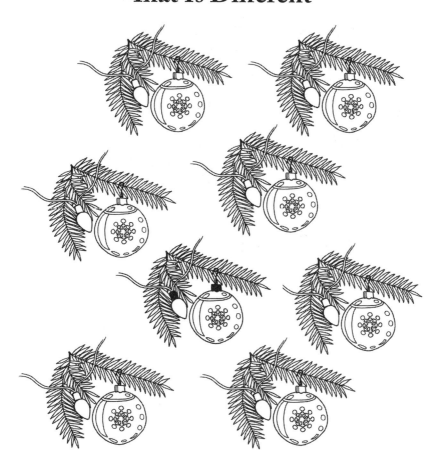

Can You Find Your Way Through the Bell?

start

finish

How Many Words Can You Make from the Words
CHRISTMAS COOKIES?

_____   _____

_____   _____

_____   _____

_____   _____

_____   _____

_____   _____

_____   _____

_____   _____

_____   _____

Read the Story of Jesus

Mary had a baby boy and named Him Jesus. He would save people from their sins. After He lived a perfect life, Jesus died for you. After being dead for three days, He was raised to life for you, and then He went back to heaven where He is now sitting in the place of honor at God's right hand, pleading for you! When everything is ready, Jesus will come and get you, so that you will always be with Him.

MATTHEW 1:21; ROMANS 8:34; JOHN 14:3

Christmas Tic-Tac-Toe

Color the Shepherds

When the angels had left them and gone into heaven, the
shepherds said to one another, "Let's go to Bethlehem and see
this thing that has happened, which the Lord has told us about."
LUKE 2:15 NIV

Unscramble the Gifts Given to Jesus by the Wise Men

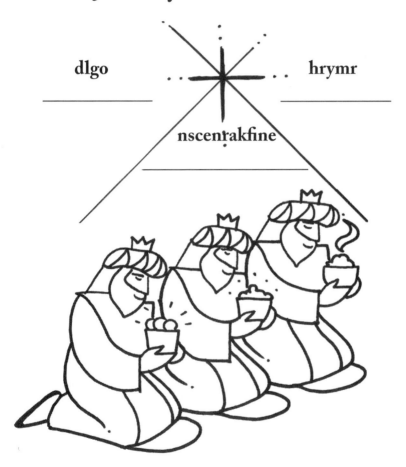

dlgo

hrymr

nscenrakfine

Find Your Way through the Maze to Get the Christmas Tree Home

Color by Number

1–red   3–yellow   5–purple   7–blue
2–green   4–brown   6–tan   8–orange

Color the Star Yellow
Color the Ornament Red
Color the Tree Green

Circle the One That Is Different

Decorate the Room
to Look Festive

ANSWER KEY

WHAT DO YOU KNOW?

A Girl Named Mary

Mary was not just any young woman. God chose her to be the mother of the Christ Child. When God spoke to her, she was willing to do whatever He asked of her. Can you answer these questions?

Who did God send to Galilee to speak to Mary about the baby she would be having? The answer is hidden in Luke 1:26.

The angel Gabriel

 Who was Mary engaged to when the angel spoke to her? The answer is hidden in Luke 1:27.

Joseph

Who was the father of Joseph, the husband of Mary, who was Jesus' mother. The answer is hidden in Matthew 1:16.

Jesus

The angel also told Mary to name her son Jesus, but He would also be called what? The answer is hidden in Luke 1:35

The Son of God

195

HOLIDAY SONGS

Find the missing word from the list below and finish the sentance

WINTER WONDERLAND

GOOD KING WENSELAS

AWAY IN A MANGER

HAPPY HOLIDAYS TO YOU

WHILE SHEPHERDS WATCHED THEIR FLOCKS

MANGER HOLIDAYS KING
SHEPHERDS WONDERLAND

196

 ## WHAT DO YOU KNOW?

Jesus Is Born

When Jesus was born, Mary and Joseph were not at their home or even in their own city. Can you answer these questions about their journey to Bethlehem?

What powerful king said that everyone had to be registered in the cities where they were born? The answer is hidden in Luke 2:1.

Caesar Augustus

Mary and Joseph went to Bethlehem because Joseph was a descendant of what great king? The answer is hidden in Luke 2:4

King David

Mary had her baby while they were on their trip. Why did she wrap up her new baby and lay Him in a manger filled with hay? The answer is hidden in Luke 2:7.

There weren't any rooms so they had to stay in the barn or stable.

197

PICTURE THIS

Draw a line from each picture to its matching word in the middle. When you are through, a few words will be left over. Fill them into the line below to form a phrase.

mistletoe

Under

christmas tree

baby Jesus

candle

bells

the

Under   the   mistletoe

199

✳ THANKSGIVING SONGS ✳

Find the missing word from the list below and finish the sentance

NOW THANK WE ALL OUR GOD

COME, YE THANKFUL PEOPLE COME

WE GATHER BLESSINGS

WITH THANKFUL HEARTS, O LORD WE COME

COUNT YOUR BLESSINGS

PEOPLE   BLESSINGS   GOD

TOGETHER   THANKFUL

200

WHAT DO YOU KNOW?

The Shepherd's Joy

On the night Jesus, the Christ Child, was born, some shepherds were up in the hills taking care of their sheep. All of a sudden, the sky lit up. Can you answer these questions?

Who appeared in the sky and told them not to be afraid? The answer is hidden in Luke 2:9.

An angel of the Lord

The angel told the shepherds that a baby had been born. What did the angel call the baby? The answer is hidden in Luke 2:11.

A Savior, who is Christ the Lord.

The angels told the shepherds where they could find the Baby Jesus. Where did they say He would be lying? The answer is hidden in Luke 2:12.

Lying in a manger.

201

WHAT DO YOU KNOW?

The Shepherds Find the Baby

When the angels finished their singing, the shepherds were filled with joy. Can you answer these questions?

What did the shepherds do when the angels disappeared? The answer is hidden in Luke 2:15.

They quickly decided to go to Bethlehem and find the Baby.

What did the shepherds do on their way home? The answer is hidden in Luke 2:20.

They went out and told everyone about the angels and the Christ Child.

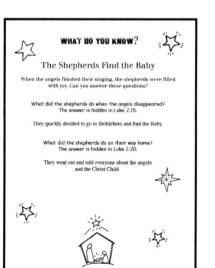

203

WHAT DO YOU KNOW?

Naming the Baby

Mary and Joseph did everything they could for their new baby. Can you answer these questions?

When Jesus was eight days old, what did His parents name Him? The answer is hidden in Luke 2:21.

They named Him Jesus.

Where did Mary and Joseph take their new son a few days later? The answer is hidden in Luke 2:22.

They went to Jerusalem to present Jesus to the Lord.

What else did Mary and Joseph do while they were in Jerusalem? The answer is hidden in Luke 2:24.

They offered a sacrifice.

204

GIVING THANKS

Fill in the missing letters to form a word or phrase from top to bottom.

F EAST
INDI_ANS
CR ANBERRIES
S WEETPOTATOES
SWEE T CORN
T URKEY
PLYMOUT H
MA Y FLOWER
BEA _ S
PUMP K INPIE
S TUFFING
VE G ETABLES
FAM I LY
HAR V EST
SHAR I NG
ACOR N
PIL G RIMS

205

Going to the Temple

Mary and Joseph made sure to dedicate Jesus to the Lord. Can you answer these questions?

Who did Mary and Joseph meet in the Temple in Jerusalem? The answer is hidden in Luke 2:25.

A man named Simeon.

What did Simeon do when he saw the Baby Jesus? The answer is hidden in Luke 2:28.

He took Jesus in his arms and blessed God for Him.

Simeon told Mary and Joseph that Jesus would be great and save us all. What did they do when they heard these words? The answer is hidden in Luke 2:33.

Mary and Joseph marveled at what Simeon said about Jesus.

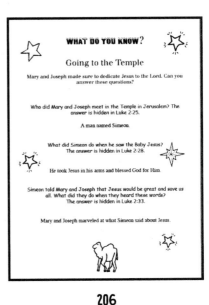

206

Everyone Loves Snow

B	S	H	O	V	E	L	M
O	H	S	A	W	O	L	P
A	O	K	W	E	P	A	S
R	E	D	N	U	O	B	T
D	N	M	L	F	J	N	O
F	L	A	K	E	A	U	R
P	A	N	G	E	L	L	M
W	H	I	T	E	N	R	L

ball   flake   shovel
board   man   storm
bound   plow   angel
fall   shoe   white

207

THE HOLY BIRTH

ACROSS

7. This is where Mary placed the new-born king
8. This is the name of Jesus' mother
9. This is the name of Jesus' earthly father

DOWN

1. The wise men followed a _____
2. Mary rode to Bethlehem on a _____
3. There were no rooms so the baby was born in a _____
4. Mary and Joseph named the baby _____
5. There were _____ in the stable
6. The shepherds and wise men were looking for the _____

208

WHAT DO YOU KNOW?

Also in the Temple

After Simeon blessed Jesus and told His parents about Him, they met a woman named Anna. Can you answer these questions?

How old was the woman Joseph and Mary met in the Temple? The answer is hidden in Luke 2:37.

Anna was 84 years old.

What did this woman do all day? The answer is hidden in Luke 2:37.

Anna served God by praying and fasting.

What did Anna do when she saw Jesus? The answer is hidden in Luke 2:38.

Anna gave thanks to the Lord for Jesus.

209

PICTURE THIS

Draw a line from each picture to its matching word in the middle. When you are through, a few words will be left over. Fill them into the line below to form a phrase.

God

snowman

Christmas tree

Thanks

gingerbread house

bells

to

Thanks ___ to ___ God ___

210

HOLIDAY SONGS

Find the missing word from the list below and finish the sentance.

IT'S THE MOST WONDERFUL TIME OF THE YEAR

WHAT CHILD IS THIS?

GO TELL IT ON THE MOUNTAIN

DECK THE HALLS

JOY TO THE WORLD

CHILD   HALLS   WORLD
MOUNTAIN   WONDERFUL

211

WHAT DO YOU KNOW?

Who Is Jesus

Jesus, the Christ Child is the most important person in all the Bible. Long before He was born, God told people about Him. Can you answer these questions?

What name did God give to Jesus? The answer is hidden in Isaiah 7:14.

Immanuel

What does the Bible say will be upon Jesus shoulders? The answer is hidden in Isaiah 9:6.

The government

What tribe or clan does the Bible say Jesus will come from? The answer is hidden in Micah 5:2.

Judah

212

Staying Warm

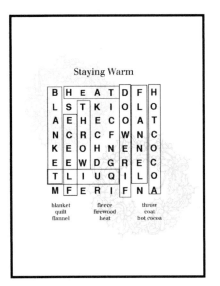

B	H	E	A	T	D	F	H
L	S	T	K	I	O	L	O
	E	H	E	C	O	A	T
A	C	R	C	F	W	N	C
N	E	O	H	N	E	N	O
K	E	W	D	G	R	E	C
E	E	D	G	R	I	L	O
T	L	I	U	Q	I	L	O
M	F	E	R	I	F	N	A

blanket   fleece   throw
quilt   firewood   coal
flannel   heat   hot cocoa

213

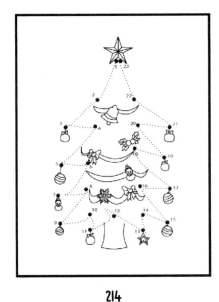

214

THE ANGEL'S SONG

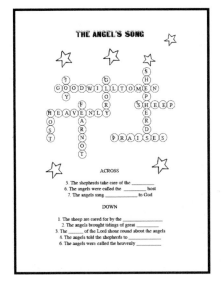

ACROSS

5. The shepherds take care of the _____
6. The angels were called the _____ host
7. The angels sang _____ to God

DOWN

1. The sheep are cared for by the _____
2. The angels brought tidings of great _____
3. The _____ of the Lord shone round about the angels
4. The angels told the shepherds to _____
6. The angels were called the heavenly _____

215

WHAT DO YOU KNOW?

The Christ Child

Can you answer these questions about the Christ Child?

Long before Jesus was born, God gave Him many titles.
Can you name give of them hidden in Isaiah 9:6?

Wonderful
Counselor
Mighty God
Everlasting Father
Prince of Peace

When will God's Kingdom end? The answer is hidden in Isaiah 9:7.

His Kingdom will have no end.

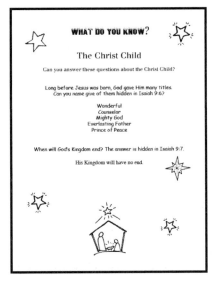

216

WHAT DO YOU KNOW?

The Three Kings

Can you answer these questions about the three kings who came to visit the Christ Child?

These kings came to Jerusalem from faraway in the East. How did they find their way? The answer is hidden in Matthew 2:2.

They followed a star.

What did the three kings do when they found Jesus? The answer is hidden in Matthew 2:11.

They fell down and worshipped the Baby Jesus

What gifts did the three kings bring to Jesus? The answer is hidden in Matthew 2:11.

Gold, frankincense, and myrrh.

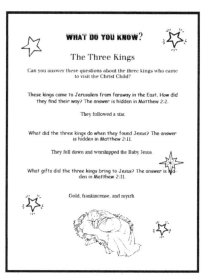

217

HOLIDAY CHEER

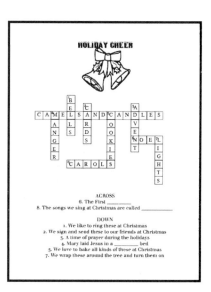

ACROSS
6. The First _____
8. The songs we sing at Christmas are called _____

DOWN
1. We like to ring these at Christmas
2. We sign and send these to our friends at Christmas
3. A time of prayer during the holidays
4. Mary laid Jesus in a _____ bed
5. We love to bake all kinds of these at Christmas
7. We wrap these around the tree and turn them on

219

PICTURE THIS

Draw a line from each picture to its matching word in the middle. When you are through, a few words will be left over. Fill them into the line below to form a phrase.

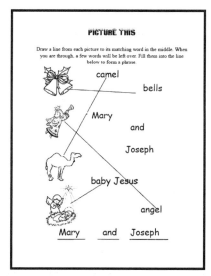

camel

bells

Mary

and

Joseph

baby Jesus

angel

Mary   and   Joseph

220

HOLIDAY SONGS

Find the missing word from the list below and finish the sentence.

IT'S BEGINNING TO LOOK A LOT LIKE CHRISTMAS

I HEARD THE BELLS ON CHRISTMAS DAY

LITTLE DRUMMER BOY

FELIZ NAVIDAD

O CHRISTMAS TREE

DRUMMER   FELIZ   CHRISTMAS

HEARD   LOOK

221

WHAT DO YOU KNOW?

Winter in the Bible

The Bible has a lot to say about wintertime.
Can you answer these questions?

What is as refreshing as a faithful messenger?
The answer is hidden in Proverbs 25:13.

Faithful messengers are as refreshing as
the cold of snow in the time of harvest.

What is it like when someone promises you a gift but doesn't give it
to you? The answer is hidden in Proverbs 25:14.

Not giving a promised gift is like
clouds and wind that don't bring rain.

What is it like when you sing a cheerful song to someone who is sad?
The answer is hidden in Proverbs 25:20.

Singing cheerful songs to a sad person is like
stealing someone's jacket in cold weather.

222

WHAT DO YOU KNOW?

Winter in the Bible

The Bible has a lot to say about wintertime. Can you answer these
questions?

The Bible says that the "coming of refreshing rain in winter" is like
what? The answer is hidden in Hosea 6:3.

Knowing the Lord.

The Bible says the "cold" comes from where? The answer is hidden
in Job 37: 9.

The scattering winds of the north.

The Bible says "ice" comes from where?
The answer is hidden in Job 37:10.

The breath of God.

223

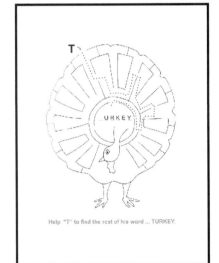

Help "T" to find the rest of his word ... TURKEY.

224

MARY'S MIRACLE

Fill in the missing letters, and the circled letters will form a word or
phrase from top to bottom.

This reindeer has a quick temper!

JE(S)US

NAT(I)VITY

ANGE(L)S

SHEPH(E)RDS

DO(N)KEY

S(T)AR

A(N)IMALS

K(I)NGOFKINGS

MA(N)GER

JOSEP(H)

BIR(T)H

225

HOLIDAY SONGS

Find the missing word from the list below and finish the sentance.

HAVE YOURSELF A MERRY LITTLE CHRISTMAS

ANGELS WE HAVE HEARD ON HIGH

GOD REST YE MERRY GENTLEMEN

O COME ALL YE FAITHFUL

THE FIRST NOEL

FIRST   REST   FAITHFUL
MERRY   ANGELS

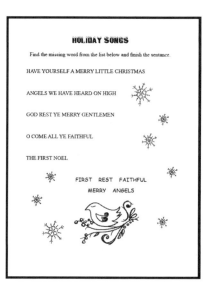

226

WHAT DO YOU KNOW?

Winter in the Bible

The Apostle Paul was arrested and sent to Rome on a ship where he would be put on trial. High winds and winter storms made the trip very dangerous. Can you answer these questions about Paul's winter journey?

Where did the ship finally stop?
The answer is hidden in Acts 27: 7-8.

A place called Fair Havens, near the city of Lasea.

When they left Fair Havens, Paul's ship set sail for what harbor in Crete? The answer is hidden in Acts 27: 12.

Phoenix, a harbor of Crete.

Everyone was afraid when the ship started to sink. What did Paul tell the frightened men who were on the ship with? The answer is hidden in Acts 27:22.

The ship would sink but all the people on board would be safe.

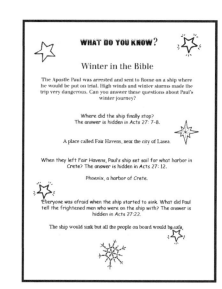

227

JOSEPH'S JOURNEY

Fill in the missing letters, and the circled letters will form a word or phrase from top to bottom.

This reindeer has a long tail

M A G I
E GYPT
HE R OD
NO R OOM
DONKE Y
CHRISTC HILD
S HEPHERDS
MAR Y
BI RTH
ANGEL S
S T AR
E M MANUEL
NA TIVITY
JE S US

228

PICTURE THIS

Draw a line from each picture to its matching word in the middle. When you are through, a few words will be left over. Fill them into the line below to form a phrase.

holiday bells

Christmas tree

and

bows

Boxes

turkey

dove

Boxes   and   bows

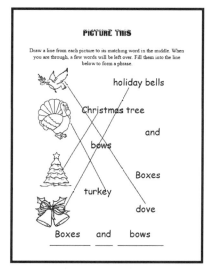

229

WHAT DO YOU KNOW?

Winter in the Bible

The wind can be very cold in the winter time. Can you answer these questions about the wind?

When the winter winds and rain beat against the house built on the rock, did it fall or did it stand strong? The answer is hidden in Matthew 7:25.

It stood strong.

When the tall waves and winter wind started to sink the boat Jesus and His disciples were sailing in, Jesus stood up and spoke to the storm. What did Jesus say? The answer is hidden in Mark 4:37-38.

Jesus said, "Peace be still."

Where does the Bible say that God walks? The answer is hidden in Psalm 104:3.

God walks on the wings of the wind.

230

ALL THE WAY

Fill in the missing letters to form a word or phrase from top to bottom.

J OLLY

RING I NG

s N o w

SLEI G H

L IGHTS

onE HORSE

B OBTAIL

opE N

L AUGHTER

FIE L DS

S ONGS

232

PICTURE THIS

Draw a line from each picture to its matching word in the middle. When you are through, a few words will be left over. Fill them into the line below to form a phrase.

snowflake

holly   tree

the

Gifts

toys

under

wise men

Gifts under the tree

233

 ## WHAT DO YOU KNOW?

Winter in the Bible

The Bible has a lot to say about wintertime. Can you answer these questions?

The Bible names five kinds of "weather." Can you name them? The answer is hidden in Psalm 148:8.

Fire
Hail
Snow
Clouds
Stormy wind

What did all these types of weather do? The answer is hidden in Psalm 148:8.

God uses them to fulfill His Word

235

THANKSGIVING GRACE

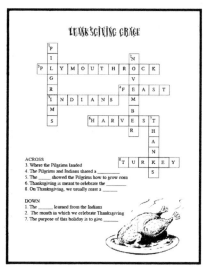

```
        P
        I
P  L  Y  M  O  U  T  H  R  O  C  K
        G              O
        R              V
        I  N  D  I  A  N  S        F  E  A  S  T
        M              M
        S        H  A  R  V  E  S  T
                        R        H
                                 A
                                 N
                        T  U  R  K  E  Y
                                 S
```

ACROSS
3. Where the Pilgrims landed
4. The Pilgrims and Indians shared a _____
5. The _____ showed the Pilgrims how to grow corn
6. Thanksgiving is meant to celebrate the _____
8. On Thanksgiving, we usually roast a _____

DOWN
1. The _____ learned from the Indians
2. The month in which we celebrate Thanksgiving
7. The purpose of this holiday is to give _____

WHAT DO YOU KNOW?

Winter in the Bible

The Bible uses snow to describe the whitest white of all. Can you answer these questions about things that are "as white as snow"?

What does the Bible say was "white as snow"? The answer is hidden in Daniel 7:9.

His garment.

What does the Bible say shall be as "white as snow"? The answer is hidden in Isaiah 1:18.

Our sins.

What does the Bible say God will do to make us "whiter than snow"? The answer is hidden in Psalm 51:7.

Wash me.

FAMILY FUN

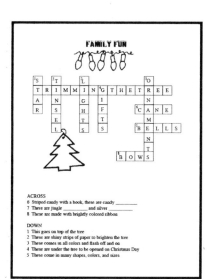

```
 S     T     L              O
 T  R  I  M  M  I  N  G  T  H  E  T  R  E  E
 A     N     G     I        N
 R     S     H     F        C  A  N  E
       E     T     T
       L     S        B  E  L  L  S
                         N
                         T
                   B  O  W  S
```

ACROSS
6 Striped candy with a hook, these are candy _____
7 There are jingle _____ and silver _____
8 These are made with brightly colored ribbon

DOWN
1 This goes on top of the tree
2 These are shiny strips of paper to brighten the tree
3 These come in all colors and flash off and on
4 These are under the tree to be opened on Christmas Day
5 These come in many shapes, colors, and sizes

PICTURE THIS

Draw a line from each picture to its matching word in the middle. When you are through, a few words will be left over. Fill them into the line below to form a phrase.

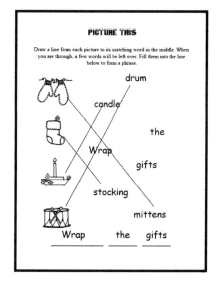

drum

candle

the

Wrap

gifts

stocking

mittens

Wrap   the   gifts

WHAT DO YOU KNOW?

Winter in the Bible

The Bible has a lot to say about wintertime. Can you answer these questions?

The Bible says the "snow" is like what?
The answer is hidden in Psalm 147:16.

Wool.

In the same Psalm, the Bible says the "frost" is like what?
The answer is hidden in Psalm 147:16.

Ashes.

What is it God says to the "snow"? The answer is hidden in Job 37:9.

Fall on the earth.

240

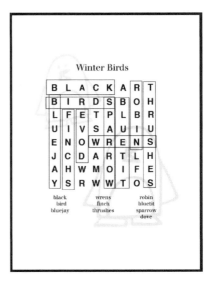

Winter Birds

B	L	A	C	K	A	R	T
B	I	R	D	S	B	O	H
L	F	E	T	P	L	B	R
U	I	V	S	A	U	I	U
E	N	O	W	R	E	N	S
J	C	D	A	R	T	L	H
A	H	W	M	O	I	F	E
Y	S	R	W	W	T	O	S

black   wrens   robin
bird   finch   bluetit
bluejay   thrushes   sparrow
                          dove

241

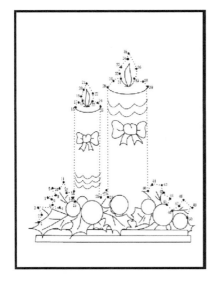

242

HOLIDAY GREETINGS

Find the missing word from the list below and finish the sentance.

CHRISTMAS IS FOR **CHILDREN**

THE CHRISTMAS **HEART** IS A GIVING HEART

GOOD **TIDINGS** OF GREAT JOY

JESUS IS THE **REASON** FOR THE SEASON

THE JOY OF CHRISTMAS BRINGS US **CLOSER** TO EACH OTHER

GOD **BLESS** US EVERYONE

BLESS   TIDINGS CLOSER
HEART   CHILDREN REASON

244

WHAT DO YOU KNOW?

Winter in the Bible

The Bible says that God is the only one who can control the weather. He decides when it will be cold and when it will be warm. Can you answer these questions?

What does the Bible say only God can do?
The answer is hidden in Job 37:3.

Send lightning to earth

What does the Bible say only God can call down from heaven?
The answer is hidden in Job 37:6.

He calls down the snow and rain

What is it the Bible says God's people are safe from even when this kind of weather comes down on them?
The answer is hidden in Isaiah 32:18-19.

Hail

245

WHAT DO YOU KNOW?

Winter in the Bible

The wind and weather are no problem for God. Can you answer these questions?

What does the Bible say God rode on when He flew upon the wings of the wind? The answer is hidden in Psalm 18:10.

A cherub.

The Bible says that dark waters and what other kind of weather was round about God? The answer is hidden in Psalm 18:11.

Thick clouds of the sky.

What does the Bible say God did in the heavens?
The answer is hidden in Psalm 18:13.

He thundered.

246

Journey of the Magi!

T	S	A	E	Z	Y	S	O
H	R	R	Y	M	R	T	S
R	E	M	N	D	O	A	T
E	M	R	S	Y	L	R	F
E	D	L	U	G	G	O	I
Y	B	A	B	D	N	A	G
S	L	E	M	A	C	I	O
S	T	A	B	L	E	M	K

camels   baby   gold
three   east   stable
kings   myrrh   gifts
                          star

247

KINGLY GIFTS

Fill in the missing letters to form a word or phrase from top to bottom.

P L A Y
K I N G
B E T H L E H E M
G I F T S
S M I L E D
B E S T
D R U M
H O N O R
P A R U M
P U M P U M
M A G I
J E S U S
P R A I S E
L A M B
S O N G
B A B Y

248

WHAT DO YOU KNOW?

Winter in the Bible

The Bible has a lot to say about wintertime.
Can you answer these questions?

Where do the "snow and rain" come from? The answer is hidden in
Isaiah 55:10.

The snow and rain come down from the heavens.

How do the "rain and snow" make the Earth better? The answer is
hidden in Isaiah 55:10.

They water the earth.
They make it bud and flourish.
They make it yield seed.

What does the Bible say is like the "rain and snow"? The answer is
hidden in Isaiah 55:11

God's Word is like the rain and snow.

249

Unscramble the Bold Letters in the Poem to Answer the Question

Whose birthday do we celebrate each Christmas?

As you celebrate
Christmas this year,

Remember Jesus
loves you dear.

251

FROM THE EAST

Fill in the missing letters to form a word or phrase from
top to bottom.

(W)ORSHIP
CAM(E)LS
ROYAL(T)Y
(H)OLY
MY(R)AH
H(E)ROD
J(E)SUS
SEE(K)
G(I)FTS
FRA(N)KINCENSE
(G)OLD
(S)TAR

252

WHAT DO YOU KNOW?

A Girl Named Mary

Mary was not just any young woman. God chose her to be the
mother of the Christ Child. When God spoke to her, she was willing
to do whatever He asked of her. Can you answer these questions?

Who did God send to Galilee to speak to Mary about the baby she
would be having? The answer is hidden in Luke 1:26.

The angel Gabriel

Who was Mary engaged to when the angel spoke to her?
The answer is hidden in Luke 1:27.

Joseph

Who was the father of Joseph, the husband of Mary,
who was Jesus' mother. The answer is hidden in Matthew 1:16.

Jesus

The angel also told Mary to name her son Jesus, but He would also
be called what? The answer is hidden in Luke 1:35

The Son of God

253

Eyewitnesses to the Birth!

A	N	N	A	Z	T	D	C
C	L	H	P	E	S	O	J
L	E	A	N	L	O	N	F
J	O	Y	E	I	H	K	O
K	N	G	S	H	E	E	P
W	N	R	M	A	R	Y	N
A	E	L	B	A	T	S	L
D	R	E	H	P	E	H	S

shepherd   angels   sheep
Anna   Mary   stable
donkeys   Joseph   hay
joy

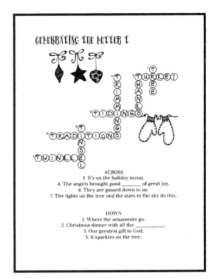

CELEBRATING THE LETTER T

ACROSS
3. It's on the holiday menu.
4. The angels brought good _____ of great joy.
6. They are passed down to us.
7. The lights on the tree and the stars in the sky do this.

DOWN
1. Where the ornaments go.
2. Christmas dinner with all the _____.
3. Our greatest gift to God.
5. It sparkles on the tree.

HOLY FAMILY

Fill in the missing letters to form a word or phrase from top to bottom.

BE T HLEHAM
JOSEP H
J E SUS
DO N KEY
M A RY
BIR T H
I NNKEEPER
TRA V EL
AN I MALS
T AXES
EG Y PT

HOLIDAY SONGS

Find the missing word from the list below and finish the sentance

WINTER WONDERLAND

GOOD KING WENSELAS

AWAY IN A MANGER

HAPPY HOLIDAYS TO YOU

WHILE SHEPHERDS WATCHED THEIR FLOCKS

MANGER HOLIDAYS KING
SHEPHERDS WONDERLAND

WHAT DO YOU KNOW?

Jesus Is Born

When Jesus was born, Mary and Joseph were not at their home or even in their own city. Can you answer these questions about their journey to Bethlehem?

What powerful king said that everyone had to be registered in the cities where they were born? The answer is hidden in Luke 2:1.

Caesar Augustus

Mary and Joseph went to Bethlehem because Joseph was a descendant of what great king?
The answer is hidden in
Luke 2:4

King David

Mary had her baby while they were on their trip. Why did she wrap up her new baby and lay Him in a manger filled with hay?
The answer is hidden in Luke 2:7.

There weren't any rooms so they had to stay in the barn or stable.

258

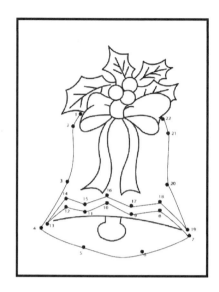

259

Celebrating the letter *H*

```
        H
    H A M
        N
        N
        U  H O P E
        K
        A
   H O L I D A Y
        H Y M N S
        E
        A
        R
        T
        S
```

ACROSS

2. It's on the holiday menu
3. Jesus' birth brings us _____
4. Christmas day is a _____
5. Carols are sometimes called _____

DOWN

1. This is a Jewish holiday
3. Green plant with small, red berries
5. God's love fills our _____

260

WHAT DO YOU KNOW?

Journey of the Wise Men

The Magi, also known as the Wise Men and the Three Kings, came looking for the Christ Child. Can you answer these questions?

What question did the Wise Men ask when they arrived in Jerusalem? The answer is hidden in Matthew 2:2.

Where is the King of the Jews?

What special sign had they followed from their homes faraway in the East? The answer is hidden in Matthew 2:2.

The star

What did they wish to do when they found the Christ Child? The answer is hidden in Matthew 2:2.

Worship Him

262

WHAT DO YOU KNOW?

The Shepherds Find the Baby

When the angels finished their singing, the shepherds were filled with joy. Can you answer these questions?

What did the shepherds do when the angels disappeared?
The answer is hidden in Luke 2:15.

They quickly decided to go to Bethlehem and find the Baby.

What did the shepherds do on their way home?
The answer is hidden in Luke 2:20.

They went out and told everyone about the angels
and the Christ Child.

264

Can you find your way
from the base of the
Christmas tree all the
way to the star?

265

WHAT DO YOU KNOW?

Naming the Baby

Mary and Joseph did everything they could for their new baby.
Can you answer these questions?

When Jesus was eight days old, what did His parents name Him?
The answer is hidden in Luke 2:21.

They named Him Jesus.

Where did Mary and Joseph take their new son a few days later?
The answer is hidden in Luke 2:22.

They went to Jerusalem to present Jesus to the Lord.

What else did Mary and Joseph do while they were in Jerusalem?
The answer is hidden in Luke 2:24.

They offered a sacrifice.

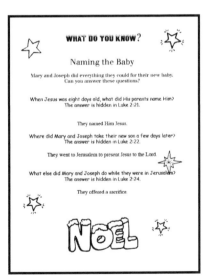

266

Songs for the Season!

```
H J A N J O Y M
F I R S T S A A
M N O E L I W N
E G Y I F L A G
D L R O W E R E
B E L L S N A R
J N I G H T T G
R E D N O W S P
```

jingle   silent   star
bells   night   wonder
away   joy   first
manger   world   noel

267

Match the Gifts with Their Shadows

WHAT DO YOU KNOW?

Going to the Temple

Mary and Joseph made sure to dedicate Jesus to the Lord. Can you answer these questions?

Who did Mary and Joseph meet in the Temple in Jerusalem? The answer is hidden in Luke 2:25.

A man named Simeon.

What did Simeon do when he saw the Baby Jesus? The answer is hidden in Luke 2:28.

He took Jesus in his arms and blessed God for Him.

Simeon told Mary and Joseph that Jesus would be great and save us all. What did they do when they heard these words? The answer is hidden in Luke 2:33.

Mary and Joseph marveled at what Simeon said about Jesus.

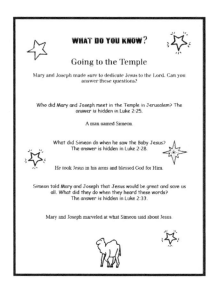

THE HOLY BIRTH

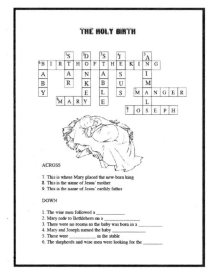

ACROSS

7. This is where Mary placed the new-born king
8. This is the name of Jesus' mother
9. This is the name of Jesus' earthly father

DOWN

1. The wise men followed a _____
2. Mary rode to Bethlehem on a _____
3. There were no rooms so the baby was born in a _____
4. Mary and Joseph named the baby _____
5. There were _____ in the stable
6. The shepherds and wise men were looking for the _____

HOLY NIGHT

Fill in the missing letters to form a word or phrase from top to bottom.

S H EPHERDS
FI E LDS
PR A ISES
SA V IOR
    E MMANUEL
FEAR N OT
ANGE L S
CIT Y OFDAVID
  C H RIST
  L O RD
MES S AGE
INFAN T

WHAT DO YOU KNOW?

Also in the Temple

After Simeon blessed Jesus and told His parents about Him, they met a woman named Anna. Can you answer these questions?

How old was the woman Joseph and Mary met in the Temple?
The answer is hidden in Luke 2:37.

Anna was 84 years old.

What did this woman do all day? The answer is hidden in Luke 2:37.

Anna served God by praying and fasting.

What did Anna do when she saw Jesus?
The answer is hidden in Luke 2:38.

Anna gave thanks to the Lord for Jesus.

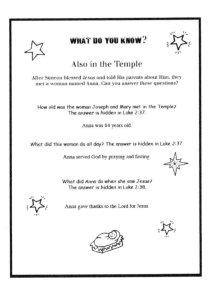

CELEBRATE THE SEASON

Fill in the missing letters to form a word or phrase from top to bottom.

```
CERE M ONY
GATHE E RINGS
MEMO R IES
SUR P RISES
TO Y S
C AROLERS
C HARITY
P RESENTS
L I GHTS
S HARING
T REE
TRI M MINGS
STA R
S TOCKINGS
```

PICTURE THIS

Draw a line from each picture to its matching word in the middle. When you are through, a few words will be left over. Fill them into the line below to form a phrase.

God

snowman

Christmas tree

Thanks

gingerbread house

bells

to

Thanks   to   God

Help the Little Mouse Get to the Christmas Star

Twinkle, Sparkle, Snowflakes Bright—Can You Find 8 Different Types?

279

Staying Warm

B	H	E	A	T	D	F	H
L	S	T	K	I	O	L	O
A	E	H	E	C	O	A	T
N	C	R	C	F	W	N	C
K	E	O	H	N	E	N	O
E	E	W	D	G	R	E	C
T	L	I	U	Q	I	L	O
M	F	E	R	I	F	N	A

blanket   fleece   throw
quilt   firewood coat
flannel   heat   hot cocoa

280

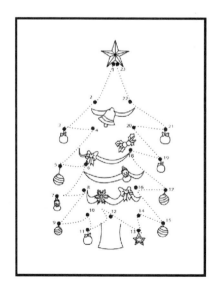

281

THE ANGEL'S SONG

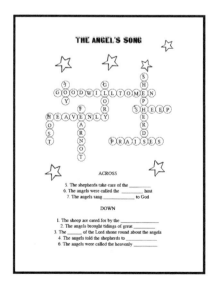

ACROSS

5. The shepherds take care of the _____
6. The angels were called the _____ host
7. The angels sang _____ to God

DOWN

1. The sheep are cared for by the _____
2. The angels brought tidings of great _____
3. The _____ of the Lord shone round about the angels
4. The angels told the shepherds to _____
6. The angels were called the heavenly _____

282

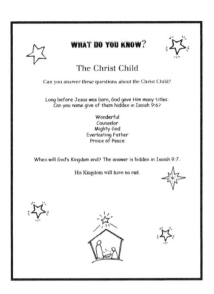

WHAT DO YOU KNOW?

The Christ Child

Can you answer these questions about the Christ Child?

Long before Jesus was born, God gave Him many titles.
Can you name give of them hidden in Isaiah 9:6?

Wonderful
Counselor
Mighty God
Everlasting Father
Prince of Peace

When will God's Kingdom end? The answer is hidden in Isaiah 9:7.

His Kingdom will have no end.

283

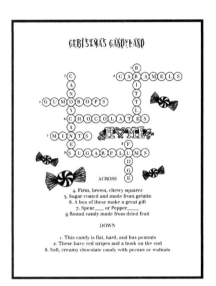

CHRISTMAS CANDYLAND

ACROSS

4. Firm, brown, chewy squares
5. Sugar coated and made from gelatin
6. A box of these make a great gift
7. Spear____ or Pepper____
9 Round candy made from dried fruit

DOWN

1. This candy is flat, hard, and has peanuts
2. These have red stripes and a hook on the end
8. Soft, creamy chocolate candy with pecans or walnuts

284

PICTURE THIS

Draw a line from each picture to its matching word in the middle. When
you are through, a few words will be left over. Fill them into the line
below to form a phrase.

reindeer

angel

Under

stocking

the

mistletoe

mittens

Under   the   mistletoe

285

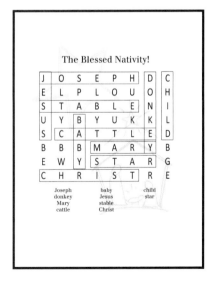

The Blessed Nativity!

J	O	S	E	P	H	D	C
E	L	P	L	O	U	O	H
S	T	A	B	L	E	N	I
U	Y	B	Y	U	K	K	L
S	C	A	T	T	L	E	D
B	B	B	M	A	R	Y	B
E	W	Y	S	T	A	R	G
C	H	R	I	S	T	R	E

Joseph   baby   child
donkey   Jesus   star
Mary   stable
cattle   Christ

287

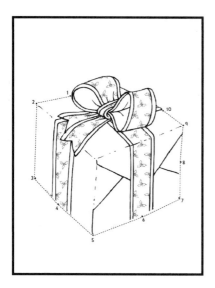

288

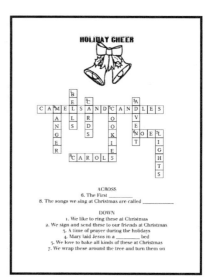

HOLIDAY CHEER

ACROSS
6. The First _____
8. The songs we sing at Christmas are called _____

DOWN
1. We like to ring these at Christmas
2. We sign and send these to our friends at Christmas
3. A time of prayer during the holidays
4. Mary laid Jesus in a _____ bed
5. We love to bake all kinds of these at Christmas
7. We wrap these around the tree and turn them on

289

PICTURE ITS

Draw a line from each picture to its matching word in the middle. When you are through, a few words will be left over. Fill them into the line below to form a phrase.

camel

bells

Dream

of

Christmas tree

snow

angel

Dream   of   snow

290

WHAT DO YOU KNOW?

Winter in the Bible

The Bible has a lot to say about wintertime.
Can you answer these questions?

What is as refreshing as a faithful messenger? The answer is hidden in Isaiah 55:13.

Faithful messengers are as refreshing as the cold of snow in the time of harvest.

What is it like when someone promises you a gift but doesn't give it to you? The answer is hidden in Isaiah 55:14.

Not giving a promised gift is like clouds and wind that don't bring rain.

What is it like when you sing a cheerful song to someone who is sad? The answer is hidden in Isaiah 55:20.

Singing cheerful songs to a sad person is like stealing someone's jacket in cold weather.

291

Holiday Pies!

```
M  A  E  R  C  E  C  I
Q  S  B  E  R  R  Y  S
R  H  U  B  A  R  B  F
A  T  T  S  R  L  I  N
P  L  R  E  I  S  S  A
P  I  H  C  A  E  P  C
L  C  R  E  A  M  L  E
E  N  I  K  P  M  U  P
```

ice cream	apple	cherry
peach	rhubarb	cream
pecan	berry	pumpkin

BOXES AND BOWS

ACROSS

2. Rushing from store to store
4. These make beautiful bows
6. Put this around the gifts to keep them hidden
7. These tell us who the gift is for

DOWN

1. Use these to cut the paper
5. Gifts are also called _____
5. This sticky stuff keeps the paper in place

WHAT DO YOU KNOW?

Winter in the Bible

The Bible has a lot to say about wintertime. Can you answer these questions?

The Bible says that the "coming of refreshing rain in winter" is like what? The answer is hidden in Hosea 6:3.

Knowing the Lord.

The Bible says the "cold" comes from where? The answer is hidden in Job 37:9.

The scattering winds of the north.

The Bible says "ice" comes from where? The answer is hidden in Job 37:10.

The breath of God.

Christmas Joy!

```
K  O  T  I  N  S  E  L
E  T  A  R  O  C  E  D
M  R  L  I  G  H  T  S
Y  S  T  F  I  G  O  T
I  B  D  R  S  C  Y  A
P  Z  Y  T  E  B  S  N
C  D  A  N  G  E  L  D
O  R  N  A  M  E  N  T
```

tinsel	stand	ornament
decorate	gifts	tree
lights	star	fir
		angel

Find These Things
You Would See in a Stable—
Each Word Is Hidden 2 Times

Hay • Manger • Cow • Sheep • Chicken • Donkey

```
A B I M S H E E P E S R O O U
U A R A W A H A R R I P G S S
S R D O N K E Y S R E E O P R
T R C A T F R A N E N G L S E
S C C O L L R N H G I K N S M
M A N G E R E S R N N I R A M
I A M A D K I H H A Y I I P M
Y I O L C V D E S M N T N I R
A A P I V C H I C K E N D R Q
L I H R W O C H H E N S S A D
H C P P S P I P E Y E K N O D
```

297

Celebrating the Letter *W*

ACROSS
2. Another word for blizzard
2 When you feed it, it fills the room with warmth
5. How cold it is when the wind is blowing
6. Snow and sleet are _____ weather

DOWN
1. In winter, we must watch the _____
2. What you would wear to stay warm
4. The cold feels even colder when it's _____

300

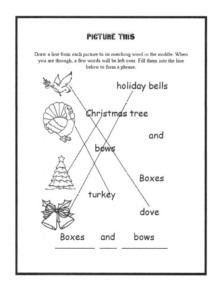

PICTURE THIS

Draw a line from each picture to its matching word in the middle. When you are through, a few words will be left over. Fill them into the line below to form a phrase.

holiday bells

Christmas tree

and

bows

Boxes

turkey

dove

Boxes   and   bows

_____   _____   _____

301

O Christmas Tree!

```
A N G E L L S G
R A T S Y O T I
B G I N T S A F
O R N A M E N T
K F S M Z W D S
Z E E R T R I F
G H L I G H T S
E T A R O C E D
```

tinsel   decorate   star
gifts   lights   angel
stand   ornament   fir tree
              toys

302

PICTURE THIS

Draw a line from each picture to its matching word in the middle. When
you are through, a few words will be left over. Fill them into the line
below to form a phrase.

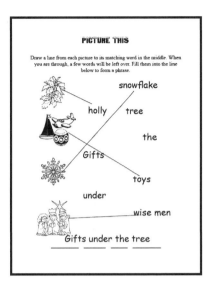

snowflake

holly   tree

the

Gifts

toys

under

wise men

Gifts under the tree
_____ _____ _____ _____

304

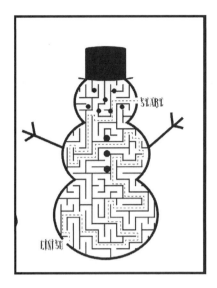

START

FINISH

306

THANKSGIVING CRAZE

ACROSS
3. Where the Pilgrims landed
4. The Pilgrims and Indians shared a _____
5. The _____ showed the Pilgrims how to grow corn
6. Thanksgiving is meant to celebrate the _____
8. On Thanksgiving, we usually roast a _____

DOWN
1. The _____ learned from the Indians
2. The month in which we celebrate Thanksgiving
7. The purpose of this holiday is to give _____

307

Winter Sport Word Search

```
G B W P C T B L N Z F G G R Y
A N O P R D K N T R N I N U F
B T I C E F I S H I N G I S I
W O T T E Y K G L S L L D L P
N X B O A E E I A M Q W R E V
Z N N S L K B K E Z Q Z A D L
R N Q E L O S X C J H X O D V
R G T N M E P E U O X A B I E
F O T W N G I S R P H V W N T
N R O Y H U G G Y U Y A O G Z
G N R Y A L Z L H H G O N Z W
S B G W K B S M X T F I S N N
U S P W K F H J J E U W F C J
K S V U Q Q H A L G N I T K S
H O Q L X C C X C T N B A W
```

308

One is different in each row. Circle the one that is different.

1.

2.

3.

309

The Shepherd's Glory!

H	P	W	K	S	T	A	R
O	E	F	I	E	L	D	E
S	E	A	L	C	J	L	G
T	H	N	V	A	O	I	N
H	S	G	E	E	Y	H	A
G	N	E	S	P	N	C	M
I	M	L	N	O	E	L	Q
N	T	S	I	R	H	C	Y

heavenly   night   joy
host   christ child   noel
field   manger   sheep
                angels

310

FAMILY FUN

¹S	²T	³L								⁵O	
T	R	I	M	M	I	N	⁴G	T	H	E	T	R	E	E
A	N	G				I				N	
R	S	H	F			N				⁶C	A	N	E
	E	T	T			S				M	
	L	S	S				⁸B	E	L	L	S
										N	
						⁷B	O	W	S		T

ACROSS
6 Striped candy with a hook, these are candy _____
7 There are jingle _____ and silver _____
8 These are made with brightly colored ribbon

DOWN
1 This goes on top of the tree
2 These are shiny strips of paper to brighten the tree
3 These comes in all colors and flash off and on
4 These are under the tree to be opened on Christmas Day
5 These come in many shapes, colors, and sizes

311

PICTURE THIS

Draw a line from each picture to its matching word in the middle. When
you are through, a few words will be left over. Fill them into the line
below to form a phrase.

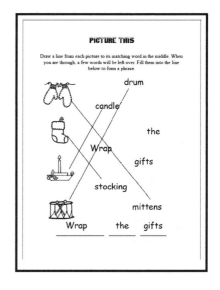

drum

candle

the

Wrap

gifts

stocking

mittens

Wrap   the   gifts
_____   _____ _____

312

Winter Sports Sudoku

313

Celebrating the Letter *G*

ACROSS
2. A cake made with molasses and ginger
5. Season's _____
7. During the holidays, we exchange _____

DOWN
1. A kindly feeling
2. Rope of flowers, greens, or tinsel
3. A string of greenery
4. Those who visit our homes are _____
6. A Dr. Seuss character

315

MOTHER AND CHILD

Fill in the missing letters, and the circled letters will form a word or phrase from top to bottom.

GOD**S**ON
VIRG**I**N
ANGE**L**S
SHEPH**E**RDS
MA**N**GER
NA**T**IVITY
NOEL
K**I**NG
MA**G**I
HOPE
MAJES**T**Y

316

PICTURE THIS

Draw a line from each picture to its matching word in the middle. When you are through, a few words will be left over. Fill them into the line below to form a phrase.

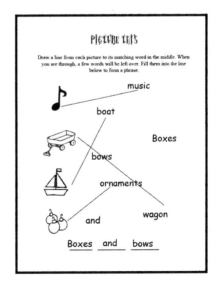

music

boat

Boxes

bows

ornaments

and

wagon

Boxes and bows

317

Circle the One That Is Different

319

The Angels' Glory

G	N	I	S	I	A	R	P
L	S	O	B	N	W	N	I
M	P	O	N	H	I	G	H
H	E	A	V	E	N	L	Y
O	A	D	K	K	G	O	D
S	C	R	V	N	S	R	L
T	E	S	H	O	L	Y	T
G	A	B	R	I	E	L	W

heavenly   on high   God
host   Gabriel   peace
praising   wings   holy

320

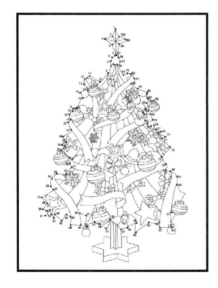

322

SURVIVING WINTER

Fill in the missing letters, and the circled letters will form a word or phrase from top to bottom.

Ⓢ CARVES
SWEAT Ⓔ RS
H Ⓐ TS
SUNN Ⓨ DAYS
F Ⓘ REPLACE
LO Ⓝ GJOHNS
LEG Ⓖ INGS
Ⓦ OODSTOVE
BL Ⓐ NKETS
EA Ⓡ MUFFS
Ⓜ ITTENS

323

Find 7 Hearts in This Picture

325

What's Different?

326

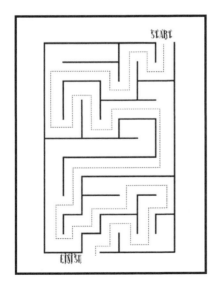

327

KINGLY GIFTS

Fill in the missing letters to form a word or phrase from top to bottom.

P L A Y
K I N G
B E T H L E H E M
G I F T S
S M I L E D
B E S T
D R U M
H O N O R
P A R U M
P U M P U M
M A G I
J E S U S
P R A I S E
L A M B
S O N G
B A B Y

328

Follow the Path

Write the number of the path in the box below.

Crossword

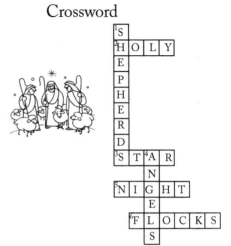

		¹S			
	²H	O	L	Y	
		E			
		P			
		H			
		E			
		R			
		D			
	³S	T	⁴A	R	
			N		
	⁵N	I	G	H	T
			E		
	⁶F	L	O	C	K	S
			S		

333

335

Find Your Way through the Maze

start   finish

337

Find Your Way through the Maze

start

338

Crossword

Find Your Way through the Maze.

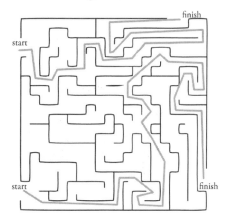

339

344

Which One Is Different?

Follow the Path
Write the number of the path in the box below.

346

349

Help the Snowman Catch
SNOWFLAKES
Catch the letters and unscramble them on the line
below to get the snowman's message to you.

L　°E　　J　°　V°
　　　　U　　S
O　°Y　°　　U E
S　　°　　　　　O

JESUS LOVES YOU!

350

Circle the One
That Is Different

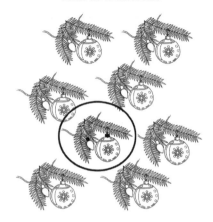

351

Can You Find Your Way
Through the Bell?

352

Unscramble the Gifts Given to
Jesus by the Wise Men

gold
frankincense
myrrh

357

Find Your Way through the Maze to Get the Christmas Tree Home

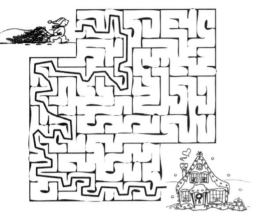

Circle the One That Is Different